Creative Working in the Knowledge Economy

There is a growing interest in the knowledge economy, and the new types of job and ways of working associated with it. This book analyses how a particular group—creative knowledge workers—carry out their jobs and learn within it. Using empirical research from advertising and software development in Europe, Singapore and Japan, it develops a new conceptual framework to analyze the complexities of creative knowledge work.

Focussing uniquely on the human element of working in the knowledge economy, it explores the real world of how people work in this emerging phenomenon and examines relationships between knowledge and creative dimensions to provide new frameworks for learning and working. It offers critical insights into how these workers apply their creative knowledge work capacities towards the production of innovative products and services, as well as using their creative abilities and knowledge to fashion both digital and tangible goods in the knowledge economy.

Adding significantly to the ongoing debate around knowledge work and creativity, this comprehensive examination will be of interest to researchers and educators in organizational learning, management and HRM and to anyone involved in devising ways to develop and support workers in lifelong and flexible creative work practices.

Sai Loo is an academic at the UCL Institute of Education, University College London. His areas of interest are in the interdisciplinary approaches to defining, identifying, and applying knowledge in different pedagogic and work settings. He has published widely including the Routledge research monograph, *Vocationalism in Further and Higher Education.*

Routledge Advances in Organizational Learning and Knowledge Management

Series Editor: Patricia Ordóñez de Pablos
University of Oviedo, Spain

Creative Working in the Knowledge Economy

Sai Loo

Routledge
Taylor & Francis Group

LONDON AND NEW YORK

First published 2017 by Routledge

2 Park Square, Milton Park, Abingdon, Oxon OX14 4RN
605 Third Avenue, New York, NY 10017

Routledge is an imprint of the Taylor & Francis Group, an informa business

First issued in paperback 2021

Library of Congress Cataloging in Publication Data
A catalog record for this book has been requested

ISBN: 978-1-138-21139-1 (hbk)
ISBN: 978-0-367-33903-6 (pbk)

Typeset in Bembo
by Apex CoVantage, LLC

To Caroline and Anna for their warm support and not forgetting the irrepressible Tosca.

And to my parents, for all they have done for me.

Contents

Figure and Tables

Figure

Tables

Acknowledgements

The journey of this research monograph has been an interesting and exciting one and there are numerous people who in one way or another have supported and guided me for which I am very grateful. They include Professor Patrick Ainley, Dr. Vincent Carpentier, Professor Andy Green, Professor David Guile, Dr. Kaori Kitagawa, Professor Hugh Lauder, Professor Prue Huddleston, Professor Ian McNay, Professor Erica Smith, and Professor Michael Young.

I would also like to thank the editors of Routledge, Clare Ashworth, Heidi Lee, Jacqueline Curthoys and Nicola Cupit in bringing this book to fruition.

Special thanks must be given to those interviewees who participated in this investigation in England, Japan, and Singapore. Their hospitality and willingness to give up their time to assist in this study were humbling for me as an investigator. I will cherish the generosities of kindness and openness, which went beyond their call of duty. I have them to thank for their professional insights in the sectors of advertising and information technology software.

1 Introduction

Setting the Context

According to Reich (2001), there are two types of creative workers with distinct personalities and talents. He says:

> The demand for creative workers—for geeks and shrinks, as I have called them—will continue to grow because they are the masters of innovation, and innovation lies at the heart of the new economy.
>
> (Reich, 2001, p. 64)

This investigation draws on Reich's description of creative workers who produce innovative goods in the knowledge economy. The roles played by these creative workers in the knowledge economy are the main focus of this study. The study was inspired by my personal life and professional work experiences. Drawing on Fuller's (1984) justification, this research was designed on the basis of my biography, although my industrial experiences were not specifically in the sectors of advertising and information technology software. As Fuller explains:

> Since what I wanted to research and how I wanted to do the research are themselves linked to my professional, personal and political biography up to that point.
>
> (Fuller, 1984, p. 98)

My interest in workers in the knowledge economy was stimulated by living in Malaysia and the UK, working as a Chartered Accountant and my academic interests. The experience of living in different parts of the world made me curious about the similarities and differences between them and led me to carrying out research on three countries: England, Japan, and Singapore. After completing a degree in Economics and a professional qualification in accountancy, I worked as a Chartered Accountant. This made me curious about the varied nature of work and how creativity influenced it, especially in advertising and IT software. As an academic in the higher education sector,

I was exposed to teaching on a variety of programmes and researching, and this practice made me query perspectives of learning and working.

A preliminary literature review made it clear that existing research on creativity was largely confined to the areas of psychology (Csikszentmihalyi, 1988; Gardner, 1993 & 1999; Sternberg, Kaufman and Pretz, 2004) and concentrated in the creative arts (Lash and Urry, 1994; National Advisory Committee on Creative and Cultural Education, 1999; DCMS, 2001). It was concluded that the emphasis on creativity by these scholars was not entirely applicable or relevant to the research questions, which this investigation hoped to answer—i.e., that of creativity in commercial environments in the contexts of a developing knowledge economy.

This realization prompted a further literature review from documentary sources (including journals, books, and reports), which linked creativity directly to work in the new economy using knowledge. Lash and Urry's (1994) research provided a connection between art-related disciplines and researchers from economics and management by Zuboff (1988), Drucker (1993), Nonaka and Takeuchi (1995) and Reich (2001) provided insights into connections of new adaptive and creative styles of working in the new economy. From psychology, Csikszentmihalyi (1988), Gardner (1999) and Sternberg et al. (2004) offered creative descriptions of knowledge work. Chapters 2, 3 and 4 discuss these creativity and workplace connections in the knowledge economy, which lead into Chapter 5 which explains the development of the theoretical framework. In fine-tuning this framework, the research of Lury (2004), von Hippel (2006), Knorr Cetina (2005a and 2005b) and Nerland (2008) were relied on. There were difficulties accessing the literature due to various reasons. These included knowing which disciplines to investigate, finding the relevant search engines to gain access to the relevant literature, and understanding the relevance and assessing the credibility of the literature to this study. These issues are illustrated by two writers. Knorr Cetina's (1997) idea of a protracted timeframe for knowledge cultures is relevant here. She argues that a new culture of creative knowledge working takes time to develop and gain acceptance by society. Similarly, Csikszentmihalyi (1988) noted that a creative idea was not a flash of inspiration but one that required time for gestation. Equally, with this investigation, it took time to seek and make connections of extant information relating to creative applications of knowledge in the new economy.

This research included a literature review as indicated above by making connections between existing information on creativity to creative knowledge work, and not investigating them separately. In order to investigate creative knowledge work as a connected area, it was suggested that a combined interdisciplinary and relational approach such as that of Guile (2010) could be more appropriate because it was more comprehensive as it drew on economics, management, psychology, and sociology. It defined the focus of the research, which was to understand how creative workers in the knowledge economy contributed towards the production of innovative goods, with an emphasis on *creative styles of working*. This included investigating the innovative application of knowledge by creative workers in the production of state-of-the-art goods in the knowledge economy.

The term knowledge economy has many definitions, but this investigation adapted the following: it is an emerging economy where information technologies such as the Internet are increasingly important in the production of goods and services, which are knowledge-based such as computer software (Quah, 1999; Castells, 2000; Reich, 2001). The justification for using this definition lay in the fact that it enabled a thorough and meaningful exploration of the abilities, skills, and personalities of creative professionals in the knowledge economy.

In order to investigate which creative abilities and knowledge were used in the production of goods in a knowledge economy, two sectors were chosen. They were chosen because the researcher wished to ascertain whether there were any variations of creativity within and between the sectors. This sectoral approach formed the main focus of the research. Three countries, England, Japan, and Singapore, were selected for investigation as it was believed that a significant characteristic of the new economy was that it was global and networked and while there could be cultural variations between countries, these were insignificant in the context of this particular research (Castells, 2000; Reich, 2001). Consequently, the selection was only relevant in so far it was important to ascertain cultural variations within the two creative work sectors.

The first professional sector, advertising, was chosen on the basis of a preliminary literature review of creativity where it was suggested that this activity embodied the essence of artistic endeavours. This was argued by scholars such as MacKinnon (1962) and Barron (1983) who had carried out studies in related areas including business, which they associated with a "conventional notion of creativity." Quah (1999), Howkins (2001) and Reich (2001) also included advertising on their lists of important sectors in the knowledge economy. Quah (1999) identifies it as an integral part of his 'intellectual property' typology, which is one of the four elements in his 'weightless economy' where goods, such as digital advertisements on the Internet, play an increasingly prominent role and have the same characteristics as knowledge. Howkins (2001) views advertising as part of an 'intangible industry' in his 'creative economy' where creative people and businesses use this intellectual property to increase product value. Reich (2001) argues that advertising executives add value to the marketplace by identifying and delivering possibilities for others. In his 'new economy' workers use their creativity to produce goods such as advertising campaigns.

The second professional sector selected was IT software because of its close relation with the knowledge economy. Academics who acknowledged its relevance and importance include Quah (1999), Castells (2000) and Reich (2001). For Quah (1999), IT is a key element in his 'weightless economy' where there is a connection between producers and consumers and where digital products, including software, are knowledge. Castells views this sector as an integral part of the infrastructure where information and communication technologies are "amplifiers and extensions of the human mind" (2000, p. 31) in the production of goods in a global and networked market. Reich (2001) argues that software engineers add value to products by identifying and developing new possibilities.

The choice of advertising and IT software as two sectors for investigation may *prima facie* appear unrelated because their working styles are quite different. Advertising is associated with the arts and creativity (Department for Culture, Media and Sport (DCMS, 2001; Howkins, 2001). Its practice is non-technical and relates to soft subjects in Arts and Humanities. Accordingly, the working style of those creative professionals in advertising is often described as artsy and unconventional in terms of work patterns and dress code. Further, it is seen to be centred around social-cultural aspects of life and society and therefore fun and entertaining (Jones, 1999; Klein, 2001; Law, 2001; Vaske, 2001; Ogilvy, 2003). In contrast, those creative workers in IT software are viewed as being highly technical and their activities are technical, scientific, and science-focussed. They are often described as "brainy," and "geeky" and lacking in communication skills. Their work is heavily reliant on IT and they work in high specification working environments. They are, generally speaking, perceived as working independently in silos and consequently functional and dry (Gates, Myhrvold and Rinearson, 1996; Torvalds and Diamond, 2001; O'Riain, 2004). The above descriptions may arguably be said to be one-dimensional. In reality, as this study aims to investigate, there are more commonalities between the two sectors than is immediately apparent. This includes, for instance, the requirement of wider types of knowledge such as cultural knowhow by IT software workers and technological knowhow by knowledge workers in advertising (Vaske, 2001; BBC News, 2007).

Working Definitions of Knowledge and Knowledge Work

During the literature review phase described above, the working definitions of concepts were considered. For the purposes of this investigation, it was decided to use an eclectic definition in order to encompass the many differing perspectives and the following were identified as important (Loo, 2011). Knowledge could be subject or non-subject related and modified by technologies. It could be explicit, as in the case of technical knowledge and communicated in writing or orally or transmitted through Internet-based software. At the same time, it could be tacit, non-communicable, and non-transmittable through technologies. Knowledge could be acquired formally, through higher education programmes or informally through interactions and experiences in workplace settings.

Knowledge work is the application of knowledge (either explicit or tacit) by a person for commercial activities (e.g., relating to innovating or creating a digital product or service) with the aid of technology (e.g., computer software and Internet) and technological objects (e.g., laptops and mobile phones). Its application is a conscious activity to create a new commercial product or service or to innovate or improve on an existing commercial product or service. This activity may be carried out individually or collaboratively or a variation of both. Like knowledge, knowledge application occurs in social contexts, both with people and technologies.

The creative dimension of knowledge work may be defined as the manipulation of knowledge using a person's skills, talents, and personalities to achieve a commercial end.

For the purposes of this study, the combination of the above definitions of knowledge work and creative dimensions in the context of the knowledge economy is called creative knowledge work or creative application of knowledge. These definitions are appropriate and relevant because they provide a starting framework to investigate: a) types of knowledge required for creative knowledge working, and b) certain specific roles of creative knowledge work in the two professional sectors.[1]

Research Questions

The refined questions included:

1. What is meant by knowledge in the 'Knowledge Economy'?

    • Why has the term 'knowledge economy' come into use?
    • What are the characteristics of this type of economy?
    • What are the sectors in the knowledge economy?
    • How is knowledge perceived?

    It should be noted that this question was posed by Guile (2010) earlier.

2. What is meant by knowledge work in the knowledge economy?

    • What are the characteristics of this way of working?
    • How have the theorists of the knowledge economy defined knowledge working?

3. How is knowledge work understood by key actors in different sectors?

    • What are some examples of knowledge working in different sectors of the knowledge economy?
    • What are the characteristics of these examples of knowledge work?

4. Is creativity an important aspect of knowledge work?

    • If so, how is creativity related to knowledge work?
    • How have the theorists of the knowledge economy viewed creativity in relation to knowledge work?
    • What are the peoples' skills, abilities, and personalities that are related to knowledge work?

5. What are the necessary contexts for creative knowledge work?

Lines of Argument of the Investigation

Characteristics of the knowledge economy include its diversity with no agreed definition, but rather a collection of perspectives which continue to evolve (Bell, 1973; Lash and Urry, 1994; Nonaka and Takeuchi, 1995; Castells, 2000; Quah, 2002; Knorr Cetina, 2005a). Any economy in transition from an industrial variety to a post-industrial variety or from the initial to more developed phases of a post-industrial economy will have unclear boundaries. This transitional process suggests that "connective dimensions" could be identified which link the old style economy to the new and they could include: a) increased digitalization of knowledge goods alongside tangible goods (Quah, 2002), b) increased global activities of business networks (Castells, 2000), and specific knowledge working of Japanese companies (Nonaka and Takeuchi, 1995) and c) closer connections between producer and user (Quah, 2002). Identification of these connective dimensions is critical because they enable an in-depth examination of the complex nature of creative knowledge working in the two sectors.

This investigation focuses on the micro level on those working in the knowledge economy and the importance of this type of study is acknowledged by Castells (2000, p. 31) who explained:

> For the first time in history, the human mind is a direct productive force, not just a decisive element of the production system.

The lines of argument consisted of:

1. The nature of work varies in the knowledge economy as it does in other economies. Some types of knowledge work require a creative approach to working, or "creative application of knowledge" or "creative knowledge work."

2. This form of knowledge work is created by a person who applies his/her knowledge for commercial activities such as the creation of new goods and/or the improvement of goods or processes. A creative knowledge worker uses his/her raw knowledge from subject-related, work-related, and life-related knowledge by manipulation, analysis, problem seeking, and problem solving to create a commercialized-targeted knowledge rich good/product. This commercialized-targeted knowledge may be different in size and capability and also in terms of relative and absolute levels of knowledge in the knowledge economy in comparison with older style economy products. One such example is the computer where the hardware decreases in size, capability improves, and memory storage and processing power increase as technology develops. The nature of work may be generic across the global and networked new economy, but it is contextualized by how knowledge is applied to specific tasks in different sectors.

3. Creative knowledge workers utilize their cognitive abilities, skills, talents, and personalities in their work to create new goods, innovate goods, or

processes and/or lead in a business environment. The types of cognitive abilities required may vary depending on the nature of the knowledge work and contexts and may also require a high standard of professional expertise. Qualifications include formal higher education degrees and professional qualifications and also informal ones such as an acute awareness of popular cultural and social trends.

4. The use of advanced technologies to assist in the manipulation of knowledge (e.g., using computer software to manipulate imagery for advertising purposes) is common in creative knowledge working. While an expertise in this may not be essential, an acute awareness of the impact advanced technologies could have on goods and end users is essential.

5. A creative knowledge worker may be involved in a closer collaboration with the end user, e.g., collaborative working on a computer software or where a creative worker is in contact with individual users, via the Internet, to improve an existing product, invent a new product, or make an existing one redundant. This closer relationship between producer and user is a new dimension in the knowledge economy.

6. The performance of creative knowledge workers is affected by enculturation which relates to a technology-based environment, life conditions such as supportive work and home environments, and academic and social knowhow. These enable creative work to be produced and acknowledged.

7. Work style in the knowledge economy could be either collaborative where an individual worker is part of a wider system including leaders or more independent, and centred around an individual worker. The requirements in terms of skills, talents, personalities, and forms of enculturation will therefore vary.

8. This investigation uses an interdisciplinary and relational approach (Guile, 2010) as it draws from circumscribed accounts of knowledge, knowledge work and creativity, and knowledge work from more than one discipline. These accounts are eclectic and discipline-centric. This interdisciplinary and relational approach will enable this investigation to develop insights into a definition of knowledge for this style of working, relationships between knowledge and creative dimension, a micro perspective of individual roles of creative knowledge working, and a conceptual framework that enables an analysis of creative knowledge working.

9. The micro perspective is focused on two sectors of advertising and IT software where there are four forms of creative knowledge working. First, the more generic forms of working in roles and functions, sectors and disciplines with little specific contexts. Second, a more nuanced understanding of forms, where there are intra-sectoral roles and functions for specific jobs. This will be elaborated by examining different jobs in the two sectors: advertising and IT software. Third, forms where jobs require different styles of work depending on the sectors: inter-sectoral type of creative knowledge work. Thus, software programme managers may have different functions when working in different organizations—e.g., a computer software company and

a multinational financial organization. The fourth form of creative knowledge work refers to the influence of these workers on the cultures they operate in. These include aspects such as the culture of 'good practice' in technical problem-solving and the 'power of expression' in software programming. These four types of creative knowledge work suggest that a micro-level investigative approach will produce a more contextualized understanding of how creative knowledge workers operate in the knowledge economy. This approach is different from that taken by Zuboff (1988), Drucker (1993), Nonaka and Takeuchi (1995) and Reich (2001) who sought to provide a more generic rather than a specific understanding of creative knowledge working. This is the main contribution of this research, in that it aims to offer a more contextualized understanding of the nature of creative knowledge working, by specific identification of forms of work in two specific sectors.[2]

Structure of the Book

The next four chapters focus on the development of a theoretical framework. Chapter 2 focuses on the knowledge economy in terms of definitions and includes a literature review of scholars such as Bell (1973), Lash and Urry (1994), Nonaka and Takeuchi (1995), Castells (2000), Quah (2002) and Knorr Cetina (2005a), who influence the definition of knowledge in the knowledge economy for this investigation. Chapter 3 covers four definitions of work in the knowledge economy by Zuboff (1988), Drucker (1994), Nonaka and Takeuchi (1995) and Reich (2001). The literature review highlights three emergent themes: individuals with their cognitive abilities, workers applying their education, training, and work experiences, and collaboration and organizational settings. Chapter 4 reviews four critical perspectives of creativity in relation to knowledge working. Three cognitive psychological thinkers are analyzed: Csikszentmihalyi (1988), Gardner (1999) and Sternberg et al. (2004), and one management, von Hippel (2006). Two themes are explored: a) workers' skills, talents, and attributes, and b) types and degrees of enculturation. Chapter 5 provides a conceptual framework for analyzing creative knowledge work using a two-dimensional matrix: styles of working (individual and collaboratively), and contexts (single and multi-context).

Chapters 6 to 9 examine the advertising and IT software sectors with reference to the five research questions and creative application of knowledge. Two chapters provide a macro perspective or a global context. The micro perspective focuses on creative application of knowledge and illustrates rich and textured examples of knowledge working, highlights the significance of ICET, provides evidence of closer collaboration between producers and users, and analyzes the enculturation process.

Chapter 10 summarises the nine previous chapters, addresses the five research questions and discusses the contributions and implications of the study from the perspectives of education and workplace practices. It concludes with suggestions for a 'Way forward.'

Chapter 11 offers succinct insights into the transferability and applicability of the findings from this investigation in notation format for potential users.

Summary

This chapter introduced the research topic, which is "Creative application of knowledge in the knowledge economy." It provided an explanation of the processes of reflection and development undergone from this initial nuanced formulation. It mapped out the research questions, the lines of argument, and the design and structure of the investigation.

It is hoped that this book will appeal to audiences at three levels:

  i) micro (individuals),
 ii) meso (organizations), and
iii) macro (societal).

It will be of interest to those with educational and professional aspirations such as managers working in organizations both work and education-related and those involved in team-building activities.

At the macro level, policy makers, education researchers, and socio-development change agents will find this investigation provides critical evidence which can be used to underpin and drive the development of new policies to encourage creativity.

Further, because this research is interdisciplinary, it is hoped that professionals and academics from business (e.g., Burton-Jones, 1999; Drucker, 1999; Howkins, 2001), economics (e.g., Cortada, 1998; Reich, 2001; Florida, 2003; Green, 2005; Martinez-Fernandez, Miles and Weyman, 2011; Jemielniak, 2012), education (e.g., Farrell and Fenwick, 2007; Brown, Lauder and Ashton, 2011), human resource management (e.g., Davenport, 2005), knowledge and organizational management (e.g., Winslow and Branmer, 1994; Alvesson, 2004; Defillippi, Arthur and Lindsay, 2006; Klein, 2008; Orr, Nutley, Russell, Bain, Hacking and Moran, 2016), sociology, psychology, and knowledge economy-related sectors—especially IT software (e.g., O'Riain, 2004; MacLennan, 2008; Nerland, 2008; Reinhardt, Schmidt, Sloep and Drachsler, 2011) and advertising (e.g., Grabher, 2004; Lury, 2004)— will find it useful, interesting, and provocative. Some of the above-mentioned references are interdisciplinary in approach and so there may be more than one related discipline as with this investigation.

Notes

1. This study is based on my doctoral research, 'Creative Knowledge Work in the Knowledge Economy.'
2. For more details of the methodology employed in this investigation, please refer to Appendix 1.

2 The Knowledge Economy and Perceptions of Knowledge

Introduction

This chapter investigates the idea of the knowledge economy and reviews existing prevalent definitions of knowledge. The aim is to explore and determine a definition of knowledge that is most appropriate for creative knowledge workers. This chapter argues that there is no one definition of knowledge and that there are differing perspectives of knowledge. It also notes that advanced technologies are important in the manipulation of knowledge especially for commercial activities. These arguments are supported by literature from economics, management, and sociology. For the purpose of this chapter, knowledge is classified as: technologically modified (by Bell, 1973; Castells, 2000; Quah, 2002) and applied (by Lash and Urry, 1994; Nonaka and Takeuchi, 1995; Knorr Cetina, 2005a).

The first section of this chapter argues that a new economy is evolving which has no defined boundaries with the previous economy. Its transitional character implies that there are connective dimensions, which link the old to the new knowledge economy. These include: increased digitalization of knowledge goods and tangible products; growth of global networks between business and culture; and closer connections between producer and user. A literature review reveals two themes in the new knowledge economy: a new approach to working and creativity to continually innovate and invent commercially seductive goods.

The second section focuses on three perspectives of technologically modified knowledge in the knowledge economy and the third section analyses three perspectives of applied knowledge. These sections do not review literature on the knowledge economy per se but to investigate relevant literature which provides a deeper understanding of the new economy and ideas about knowledge for the purposes of this investigation, which will be defined in Chapter 3. In addition, theories of individual writers that are reviewed are not meant to be exhaustive accounts but circumscribed accounts to reflect the relevance of their theories to the research questions and the lines of argument. The final section provides a summary and a review of the similarities and differences in the literature.

Technologically Modified Knowledge Perspectives

This section explores the characteristics of technologically modified knowledge in the context of the knowledge society/economy from the perspectives of three writers: Bell (1973), Castells (2000), and Quah (2002) and argues that technologies play a significant role in the way in which knowledge is manipulated.

Technologically Modified Knowledge of Science and Technology

Knowledge may be advanced in many ways, and one way is through scientific experiments in laboratories, which require the support of advanced technologies. In order for this form of disciplinary knowledge to occur, a new form of society has to exist. Bell (1973) charted the social developments from an industrial society to a post-industrial society and noted that the post-industrial society revolved around information where the axial principle was the "centrality of and codification of theoretical knowledge" (Bell, 1973, Table 1–1). He explained that it was an information exchange "game between persons" who were professionals and scientists and technicians who applied "abstract theory through the use of models, simulation, decision theory and systems analysis" (Bell, 1973, Table 1–1).

He defined knowledge:

> as a set of organised statements of facts or ideas, presenting a reasoned judgement or an experimental result, which is transmitted to others through some communication medium in some systematic form.
>
> (Bell, 1973, p. 175)

Bell distinguished knowledge from news and entertainment but not from information. He saw knowledge as new judgements where research and scholarship were required, which included new ways of presenting previous knowledge through the use of textbooks and teaching. It related to:

> the primacy of theory over empiricism, and the codification of knowledge into abstract systems of symbols that can be translated into many different and varied circumstances.
>
> (Bell, 1973, pp. 343–344)

Bell argued for knowledge which was derived from research and development in a codified form and which relied on technologies for its utilization but did not explain how scientific and technological knowledge changed the nature of work, nor did he point out that there could be other forms of knowledge which could be non-codifiable and non-scientific. He also did not indicate which new sectors of work were likely to emerge in the future and, while he acknowledged there was a change in how individuals worked, he did not explore this, or how theoretical knowledge might be modified by technology or through interaction with the consumer. The next section explores these issues.

Technologically Modified Knowledge by People Using Information, Communications, and Electronic Technologies in Global Networks

This section argues that Bell's perspective of scientific knowledge is further developed when individuals' cognitive abilities are used to manipulate knowledge towards commercial activities. These activities are supported by advanced technologies and they occur in a globalized and networked business world. Castells used Bell's (1973) concepts of economic history and knowledge as a starting basis for his critique of the emerging "new economy" (Castells, 2000, p. 77). However, his concepts diverge from Bell's in terms of the informational mode of development, and also the emergence of a new economy. He argued, in contrast to Bell, that cognitive abilities were crucial in commercial activities and not the centrality of knowledge and information. Castells explained:

> the application of such knowledge and information to knowledge generation and information processing/communication devices, in a cumulative feedback loop between innovation and the uses of innovation . . . For the first time in history, the human mind is a direct productive force, not just a decisive element of the production system.
>
> (Castells, 2000, p. 31)

He viewed knowledge, not like Bell as a discipline-based in the sciences, but as extant scientific ideas that could be encoded in digital systems and expanded exponentially. This modification using "information, communication and electronic technologies" (ICET) (Castells, 2000, p. 31) occurred in incremental stages and lead to the production of goods and services. He argued that such innovation was the result of technologies becoming "amplifiers and extensions" (Castells, 2000, p. 31) of the human mind. However, Castells did not offer details as to how his type of knowledge interfaced with production in organizations to make knowledge innovative. This investigation attempts to fill in this lacuna. Castells's emphasis on innovation implies that creative activities are an important part of work in the knowledge economy. Also implicit is the wider scope of other sectors involved in manipulation of symbols besides science and technology sectors such as culture industries (which will be discussed in more detail by Lash and Urry [1994] in the next section).

Bell's research and development-based knowledge occurred in laboratories and science-related environments for use in a post-industrial society and Castells' extant scientific knowledge was used for commercial activities in the new economy. Castells believed that the new economy was "informational, global, and networked" (2000, p. 77).

The first characteristic, informational, is explained as entities, which are dependent on their abilities to produce and use knowledge-based information. For him the global was where:

> the core activities of production, consumption, and circulation, as well as their components (capital, labour, raw materials, management, informa- tion, technology, markets) are organised on a global scale, either directly or through a network of linkages between economic agents.
>
> (Castells, 2000, p. 77)

And networked as being:

> generated through and competition is played out in a global network of interaction between business networks. This new economy emerged in the last quadrant of the twentieth century because the information technol- ogy revolution provided the indispensable, material basis for its creation.
>
> (Castells, 2000, p. 77)

These definitions suggest that global businesses in sectors such as advertising and IT software may be organized along these lines and that a 'global' approach to business is more significant than the impact of culture on creative knowledge work. The four empirical chapters will offer evidence to support this.

Castells presented interesting perspectives of knowledge in a globalized business environment but did not explain how the interface between ICET and human minds would happen in terms of a) the types of jobs involved, b) the individuals required, and c) the nature of knowledge work. He also did not sufficiently clarify how this would be different from work in the industrial economy. Castells's research, like this investigation, focused on the business world. For him, creativity was staggered and managed and not necessarily completely original. Neither was it based on new ideas or having digital products through the use of technologies. This is investigated in the next section.

Technologically Modified Knowledge of Digital Goods and Industries and a Closer Relationship between Manufacturer and Consumer

This section discusses how the production of digital knowledge requires manipulation and the assistance of advanced technologies and involves a closer working relationship between producers and end users.

Quah (1999 and 2002), an economist, defines the 'Weightless' or 'New Economy' (his choices of terms) as:

> an economy where digital goods figure prominently in determining aggre- gate economic outcomes—innovation, production and consumption.
>
> (Quah, 2002, p. 7)

Based on his understanding, economics had traditionally viewed digital goods as ideas and this historical association made it natural to relate digital goods with the production or supply side of the economy. For him, the new economy was knowledge-driven where increased productivity related to technological advances due to accumulation of knowledge. He argued that the existence of digital goods changed the way in which this new type of economy should be perceived from an economic point of view. He noted:

> that digital goods can also contribute directly to utility from their consumption by final consumers on the demand side.
>
> (Quah, 2002, p. 8 part of Figure 1 explanation)

A timeline of the evolution of work in the new economy shows that while for Bell (1973) it centred on the existence of digital goods, whereas for Quah (2002), the traditional economic approach of viewing it from a production point of view was insufficient and he argued that consumption needed to be included in the digital equation. His emphasis of digital goods suggested that there would be a massive growth in this sector and that related new sectors would also emerge which would make the manufacturer and consumer closer. It also meant that there would be a faster turnover as the time for manufacturing these new goods and making them available became shorter due to ICET, which in turn could lower costs (with the disappearance of the middle person).

For Quah (2002) a digital good:

> is a payoff-relevant bitstring, i.e. a sequence of binary digits, 0s and 1s, that affects the utility of or payoff to some individual in the economy. Easiest is to think of a digital good as a recipe.
>
> (Quah, 2002, p. 6)

Quah saw knowledge as interchangeable with digital goods and also used to create new varieties of digital goods and in this sense Quah offers a nuanced richer perspective of knowledge. Examples of digital goods include computer software, visual images, music, databases, video games, DNA sequences, and codified messages. However, certain visual images were not digital goods e.g., works of art.

This distinction was critical for him because it highlighted the idea that products from the old economies were tangible while products from the knowledge economy could be both tangible and intangible. Both needed protection of intellectual property rights. Tangible products included motor vehicles and mobile phones and intangible, digital films and e-books. Based on Quah's (2002) definition, IT software and advertisements can be classified as digital goods which could be redesigned and reassigned (like digital music recordings) or remain unchanged like computer software. Both Bell (1973) and Castells (2000) noted that innovation was a prerequisite for the production of digital goods and because it was codifiable with an economic value, it required an intellectual element and this needed protection through patent and copyright. This is relevant for IT and advertising.

Quah (2002, p. 6) provided five characteristics of "digital/weightless" goods: nonrival, "infinitely expansible, discrete, aspatial and recombinant that are similar in behaviour to knowledge or information." A good is nonrival:

> when its use by one agent does not degrade its usefulness to any other agent. Thus, ideas, mathematical theorems, video games, engineering blueprints, computer software, cookery recipes, the decimal expansion of π, gene sequences, and so on are nonrival. By contrast, food is distinctly rival: consumption renders it immediately no longer in existence.
>
> (Quah, 2002, p. 13)

It is infinitely expansible:

> when its quantity can be made arbitrarily large arbitrarily quickly at no cost. Infinite expansibility is why media companies fear that digital music and images—costly for them to produce but distributed freely over the Internet—will proliferate without bound.
>
> (Quah, 2002, p. 13)

The infinite expansibility always generated nonrivalry because every individual owned his/her own copy. This would eventually result in a market failure, as the price for the product would be zero. The other possibility is subtler where there is a nonrivalry without infinite expansibility and so quantity is restricted and the price is above zero.

A weightless good is discrete or invisible, as it can only exist as a product in integer amounts.

Digital goods are aspatial in the sense that they are nowhere and everywhere simultaneously because of how they are transported and distributed via information communication technologies like the Internet (Quah, 2002).

Finally, they are recombinant because new digital goods are made from combinations of old products like in computer software or a video. This approach cannot be applied to non-digital goods like clean air, national defence, or a lighthouse (Quah, 2002).

Quah (1999) also believed that non-additivity was critical, especially in relation to the supply of knowledge products. He explains non-additivity as:

> The production of knowledge may often take one computer programmer working intensely for a period of time. You do not necessarily get a better product or faster product by throwing more computer programmers, more software designers, more graphic artists at the particular project.
>
> (Quah, 1999, p. 28)

The nature of new digital goods indicates that the manner in which they are developed, manufactured, and marketed for consumption requires alternative working approaches from the past. Additionally, innovative/creative input was a prerequisite for the exploration of new ideas and goods, which appealed to consumers who, due to digitization, could also be involved in the manufacturing. An example is video games where an end user can not only modify and personalize game outcomes but can also share the product with other users.

In this section, knowledge was defined as being composed of digitalized sequences of binary digits and modified by technologies. It was used to form digital/intangible goods. This digitalization and modification of knowledge allowed the creation of weightless digital goods, which could be tangible or intangible and which could be produced and consumed via digital technologies such as the Internet. The goods could also be modified (e.g., digital games) and created (e.g., printed circuit CAD software) by the end user. These are codified/explicit and discipline-related areas of knowledge. While Bell, Castells, and Quah defined knowledge as codified/explicit and discipline-related in relation to technologies, none of them consider: a) the application of knowledge in other forms, b) the way in which this knowledge may relate to/be applied to other disciplines and c) knowledge that is of a non-codifiable variety. These are critical gaps in their research. The next section explores these aspects.

Applied Knowledge Perspectives

This section investigates other types of knowledge: applied knowledge perspectives relating to the knowledge economy. Running across the specific perspectives are two underlying themes relating to: a) a new way of knowledge working and b) a need for a creative dimension to make new and commercially seductive knowledge goods.

Applied Knowledge of Culture Industries and Aesthetic Sensibilities

This section argues for arts-related knowledge though this does not preclude it from having similarities with certain science/technology-related knowledge.

Lash and Urry (1994) explored the evolution of Fordism to a post-Fordism industrial structure and argued for the inclusion of culture industries in the knowledge economy. They said the movement from Fordism to post-Fordism occurred in two forms of vertical disintegration. This movement from one form of industrial system to another is in striking contrast to Bell's industrial to post-industrial society and indicates the transitional nature of an industrial economy and the knowledge economy. The first form of vertical disintegration was "downstream"; Lash and Urry use the UK publishing industry as an illustration to explain the contracting-out of services such as warehousing, invoicing, copy-editing, and designing (Lash and Urry, 1994, p. 116).

The second form was 'upstream' disintegration where authors gained influence with regard to their advances resulting in the deterioration of publishing firms' terms of trade. This was due to the rise of literary agents who in the 1980s had previously worked in these publishing firms, decided to leave and set up their own agencies. This change in the agents' business model improved their literary functions as they applied their knowledge in a crucial intermediary role in terms of vetting of books, finding books for publishers on specific topics, and nurturing potential authors (Lash and Urry, 1994). As a result of upstream disintegration, agents, besides being able to negotiate larger advances for their clients (i.e., authors), also had greater say in contract matters such as "better royalty terms, larger share of rights sales by the publisher (such as for newspaper serialization), and a better slice of the paperback deal" (Lash and Urry, 1994, p. 117).

Lash and Urry's (1994) examples of cultural industries that warranted inclusion in the knowledge economy were based on assumptions, which were not expanded. Neither was their idea of creativity explored. This will be investigated in Chapter 4. Also implicit was the different approach to applying knowledge of the culture industries in the post-Fordist/knowledge economy of flexible disintegration where continuous innovation had become *de rigueur*. However, these authors did not examine the different patterns of working, different job activities, and jobs requirements in culture industries. Differing forms of knowledge working will be investigated in Chapter 3.

Besides advocating that culture industries should be part of knowledge economy, Lash and Urry (1994) also showed that there was a close relationship between culture industries[1] such as advertising and certain technology sectors such as IT software, which they called 'aesthetic sensibility.' Chapters 6 to 9 on advertising and IT software will illustrate the creative applications of such 'aesthetic sensibilities,' culminating in generalization of the two sectors in the final chapter. They explained this relationship in the following manner:

> In the culture industries the input is aesthetic rather than cognitive in quality. Closest to the culture industries in being highly R&D intensive is the manufacture of software. But whereas the software sector entails abstract, codified knowledge, what the culture sector entails among its artists who are so important in creating the value-added is not cognitive knowledge but a hermeneutic sensibility (although video games of course entail such an aesthetic sensibility). It is to be able hermeneutically to sense, or to intuit, the semantic needs of their public.
>
> (Lash and Urry, 1994, p. 123)

This appreciation and sensitivity to beauty and good taste—aesthetic sensibilities— is also connected to branding and adding value to a product. The 'added value' is explained in the following manner:

> The notion of brand connotes image. And value-added also stems from the artist's image. In the otherwise closely related software industry, value-added stems from the author's semiotic skills and abilities. In the

culture industries, value-added results from semiotic skills as well as from image.

(Lash and Urry, 1994, p. 137)

Semiotic skills refer to the use of signs and symbols (Oxford University Press, 1990) in a particular field such as software.

In this section, knowledge of the culture industries is part of the tapestry of the knowledge economy alongside knowledge of science and technology. However, the different discipline-related knowledge may be connected through aesthetic sensibilities. By acknowledging a wider perspective of knowledge in the knowledge economy, this investigation can deepen the understanding of the impact of knowledge on knowledge work. However, this wider perspective of knowledge also begs the following questions: What are knowledge sectors? Are there commonalties between them? Are design and aesthetic appeal more crucial than science-related knowledge? Does it imply that another type of economy is emerging? These are some of the fundamental questions that ought to be asked when thinking about the inclusion of cultural sectors in the knowledge economy. The empirical chapters will offer a deeper understanding of the above questions.

Of the four writers investigated so far, the following have not been explicitly examined: the micro nature of knowledge work, the types of people needed for this work, the types of jobs within a sector and between sectors, the diverse characteristics of jobs in knowledge-based economies, and the manner in which creativity plays a major part in this style of work. This investigation will explore these further.

There are other forms of applied knowledge in businesses, which have not been explored and these are explored next.

Applied Knowledge of Tacit and Explicit Varieties in Business Organizations

This section argues that non-disciplinary and non-codifiable knowledge is relevant to the definition of knowledge in the knowledge economy. It suggests that a social approach to knowledge making is needed in business organizations.

Knowledge, as non-disciplinary and non-codifiable forms, is examined by Nonaka and Takeuchi (1995) in the following manner:

> First, knowledge, unlike information, is about *beliefs* and *commitment.* Knowledge is a function of a particular stance, perspective, or intention. Second, knowledge, unlike information, is about *action*. It is always knowledge "to some end". And third, knowledge, like information, is about *meaning.* It is context-specific and relational.
>
> (Nonaka and Takeuchi, 1995, p. 58)

One might surmise that knowledge has a human dimension, but in an organizational context it requires the ability to use it to create something with a specific context in mind.

They drew upon Polanyi's (1966) distinction of an individual's tacit and explicit knowledge in their theoretical analysis. They saw Polanyi's tacit knowledge as:

> personal, context-specific, and therefore hard to formalise and communicate. Explicit or "codified" knowledge, on the other hand, refers to knowledge that is transmittable in formal, systematic language.
>
> (Nonaka and Takeuchi, 1995, p. 59)

However, Nonaka and Takeuchi (1995) took a slightly different view of tacit and explicit knowledge and explained as follows:

> knowledge of experience tends to be tacit, physical, and subjective, while knowledge of rationality tends to be explicit, metaphysical, and objective. Tacit knowledge is created "here and now" in a specific, practical context and entails what Bateson (1973) referred to as "analog" quality. Sharing tacit knowledge between individuals through communication is an analog process that requires a kind of "simultaneous processing" of the complexities of issues shared by the individuals. This form of social approach of knowledge is different to Polanyi's. On the other hand, explicit knowledge is about past events or objects "there and then" and is oriented towards a context-free theory.
>
> (Nonaka and Takeuchi, 1995, pp. 60–61)

It is this distinction between 'corporate' tacit and explicit knowledge that Nonaka and Takeuchi (1995) argue is fundamentally different between the Western and Japanese approaches to knowledge. They posit that Western managers are more accustomed to dealing with explicit knowledge but in so doing fail to recognize the relevance of tacit knowledge in their organizations in three ways. These are as follows: one is that tacit knowledge and its associations with subjective insights, intuitions, and hunches together form an important part of knowledge. It cannot be gained through education and training but only through direct experience and trial and error. Two, on acquiring tacit knowledge, a person begins to think about innovation differently, keeping in mind a commitment to/from an organization and her/his identification with the company's goal. Consequently, new knowledge can be created only after intensive and laborious interaction among members of the organization all sharing the same vision and commitment. Three, knowledge can be learnt in less formal ways that focus on:

> highly subjective insights, intuitions and hunches that are gained through the use of metaphors, pictures or experiences.
>
> (Nonaka and Takeuchi, 1995, p. 11)

Consequently, "social knowledge" is situated in a corporate context with commercial goal(s) and has an explicit Japanese cultural dimension.

Using theories of tacit and explicit knowledge, Nonaka and Takeuchi (1995) identified four modes of knowledge conversion: a) 'socialization' from tacit knowledge to tacit knowledge, b) 'externalization' from tacit knowledge to explicit knowledge, c) 'combination' from explicit to explicit knowledge and d) 'internalization' from explicit to tacit knowledge.

The two authors viewed this four-stage-sequence as the 'knowledge spiral' in the following manner:

> the interaction between tacit knowledge and explicit knowledge (which) will become larger in scale as it moves up the ontological levels. Thus, organizational knowledge creation is a spiral process starting at the individual level and moving up through expanding communities of interaction, that crosses sectional, departmental, divisional, and organizational boundaries.
>
> (Nonaka and Takeuchi, 1995, p. 72)

Nonaka and Takeuchi present a persuasive case for the inclusion of tacit and explicit knowledge in business organizations. However, a closer analysis reveals the following. First, Nonaka and Takeuchi (1995) did not define innovation or creativity and this leads to the conclusion that they assumed the terms have universally accepted and known definitions. This is problematic because these terms are not monolithic. The four modes of knowledge conversion, which they describe, can be critiqued for being too directional and dependent on each process, right from the initial socialization stage. The third point relates to 'blue sky products' where they examine in depth case studies of group innovative practices like Honda City car model. While they provide a new approach to knowledge application, their discussion is insufficient with regard to how blue sky products (or new products that are totally different to existing company products) fit into their model, and consequently, they fail to elucidate upon the finer workings of the process of innovation. Even the authors warned of the dangers of a comprised group mentality and merely adaptation of successful products (Nonaka and Takeuchi, 1995, p. 198). In fact, it would be true to say that this form of innovation is incremental in nature and does not really deal with the blue-sky version of products.

They argued that the creative stage of externalization is the most creative process of the four modes, but they fail to explain how the process is creative and merely offer case studies as an explanation. Arguably, their contribution offers a new cultural perspective in Japanese organizations. However, it fails because this collective innovative approach may not be applicable to cultures which do not have similar homogenous characteristics. Their contribution also lacks an in depth explanation of the finer details of knowledge work and why and how creativity is a prerequisite to an innovative approach. Finally, they did not explore the idea that a knowledge economy required an "epistemic culture" (Knorr Cetina, 2005a, p. 67) before it could flourish. The next part investigates this prerequisite of an epistemic culture.

Applied Knowledge of Science and other Disciplines, Epistemic Cultures, and Objectualization

This section discusses why knowledge production may not be possible without the existence of an "epistemic culture" in an industrial society.

Knorr Cetina (2005a), a sociologist, researched "epistemic cultures" in high-energy physics and the foreign exchange market (Knorr Cetina and Bruegger, 2002a & 2002b; Knorr Cetina, 2005b). She advocated that such cultures were open to individuals and, accordingly, objects became more significant. Implicit in her examples of the two epistemic cultures is the necessity of: a) creativity in producing knowledge and the relevance of objects in the knowledge work and b) different modes of working.

She suggested that a knowledge society did not merely imply "a society of more experts, of technological infra- and information structures" (Knorr Cetina, 1997, p. 8) but one where:

> knowledge cultures have spilled and woven their tissue into society, the whole set of processes, experiences and relationships that wait on knowledge and unfold with its articulation.
>
> (Knorr Cetina, 1997, p. 8)

Indeed, her attention is focused on 'epistemic cultures' where she aims to:

> capture these interiorized processes of knowledge creation. It refers to those sets of practices, arrangements, and mechanisms bound together by necessity, affinity, and historical coincidence that, in a given area of professional expertise, make up how we know what we know. Epistemic cultures are cultures of creating and warranting knowledge.
>
> (Knorr Cetina, 2005a, p. 67)

However, she does not clarify how actual knowledge creation occurs. She discussed epistemic cultures in high-energy physics and futures trading and noted their different characteristics and implies the prerequisite for creativity, especially in high-energy physics. But to what extent and how it is applied are not explained. These gaps will be discussed in this research.

People in a technological-centred society are becoming dependent on artefacts in their daily lives. Knorr Cetina (2005b) advocated the idea of 'objectualization' in the following manner:

> the social is not limited to the human" and that in a 'postsocial' environment, objects (e.g. technologies, viruses, animals, and other natural objects) "displace human beings as relationship partners and embedding contexts or increasingly mediate human relationships, making the latter dependent on the former.
>
> (Knorr Cetina, 2005b, p. 556)

Computer software is an example where objects continually change and get updated with different versions (Knorr Cetina, 2001a). In the case of foreign exchange trading, screens depicting market prices, information, and transactions are epistemic objects (Knorr Cetina and Bruegger, 2002b). The need to have human involvement is highly relevant to my investigation, as has already been evidenced earlier in this chapter. The inclusion of objects in working lives of people and the growing reliance on the objects such as mobile phones and laptop computers provide an insight beyond the manipulation of knowledge and its application using technologies. This forms the basis of the empirical research in Chapters 6 to 9 and includes exploring the relevance and relationship between people and objects towards the eventual production of goods.

This section argued that epistemic cultures were a prerequisite for the knowledge economy and each culture had its own characteristics. People are essential to carry out work practices and are increasingly dependent on objects, which affect their knowledge work.

Summary

This chapter noted there was no one definition of knowledge in the knowledge economy but differing perspectives of knowledge and that technologies were necessary in the manipulation of knowledge. Knowledge may be derived from research and development—i.e., theoretical. Knowledge may be extant scientific and used in globalized business organizations or it may be binary digits used towards the production of digital goods. Knowledge may also be cultural such as advertising. These forms of knowledge are discipline-related and codifiable. There may be similarities between different disciplines such as aesthetic sensibilities. Knowledge may also be tacit and derived in social working environments such as business organizations and may include beliefs and people's experiences. At present, the perspectives of knowledge from the disciplines of economics, management, and sociology are discrete and unconnected.

This investigation sees these perspectives as being related as it relies on an interdisciplinary and relational approach (Guile, 2010) to provide insights into a definition of knowledge in the new economy. A definition of knowledge will be provided in the next chapter and this relational approach will be examined in Chapter 10.

There is no single definition of the knowledge economy and some of the terms used include post-industrial society, weightless economy, new economy, and post-Fordist economy. The knowledge economy is in transition from the old industrial-based economy to a new post-industrial form. This transitional process suggests there are connective dimensions, which link the old to the new. These include: the increasing digitalization of knowledge goods (e.g., music, advertisements, books, and films) due to the accelerating developments of advanced technologies (including the Internet), alongside tangible products (e.g., laptops, MPS players, and mobile phones). Within this connective dimension there are two implications. The first is that the culture industries alongside science and technology sectors should be included as part of the knowledge economy. The second is an aesthetic sensibility that is associated with certain culture industries, and science and technology such as in IT software and advertising.

The second connective dimension is the increasing global network of business and cultural perspectives. The latter is outside the remit of this investigation.

The final connective dimension relates to closer connections between the producer and users or consumers of products or services. One example is the pop group, The Arctic Monkeys (Gibson, 2005), which produces and distributes its music directly to its audience through the Internet.

Two areas that have not been explicitly discussed here are: a) the nature of working in the knowledge economy, which will be investigated in Chapter 3, and b) the creative dimension of knowledge working in Chapter 4.

Note

1. In Chapter 10, the definition of culture industries will be synonymous with the 'creative industries' definition used by the Department for Culture, Media and Sport (2001) in England.

3 Knowledge Work

Issues and Perspectives

Introduction

In the previous chapter, it was shown that the knowledge economy was in transition, and there were differing perspectives of knowledge and connective dimensions that exist between the old and new economies. These dimensions can be investigated at three levels: a) macro, which includes analysis of occupational, professional, and industrial sector classifications, b) meso, which investigates work in corporations and c) micro, which examines the nature of work. This chapter focuses on the meso and micro levels of work in different contexts (revisited in Chapter 5) of the knowledge economy.

This chapter argues there is no one approach to knowledge work and that there are different types. Commercial knowledge work requires particular skills, talents, and personalities in their application of knowledge and individuals can work either collaboratively or independently. Knowledge workers apply their education, training, and previous work experiences in their roles.

This chapter aims to provide an in depth understanding of knowledge work, rather than offer a comprehensive review of all scholarly articles in this area. Scholars highlighted in the previous chapter will be discussed here again to provide a comparative analysis on the knowledge economy and perspectives on knowledge work. The analysis offers some connecting themes, which leads to the development of the conceptual framework of creative knowledge work (presented in Chapter 5) using an interdisciplinary and relational approach (Guile, 2010).

A Literature Review of Knowledge Work

The writers reviewed in this section included Zuboff (1988), Drucker (1993), Nonaka and Takeuchi (1995) and Reich (2001). The section starts with Drucker (1994, p. 278) as he was the first to use the term "knowledge work," the others follow in chronological order.

Individuals and Technological Skills

Drucker (1999) recognized and identified a new way of working in the knowledge economy. He coined the phrase 'knowledge work' and introduced a new category of knowledge workers: 'technologists.' Drucker offers a definition of 'knowledge work' and 'knowledge worker':

> The arrival of the knowledge worker changed the nature of jobs. Because modern society has to employ people who expect and demand knowledge work, knowledge jobs have to be created. As a result, the character of work is being transformed.
>
> (Drucker, 1994, p. 278)

Drucker's (1999) significant contribution to a better understanding of knowledge working is found in his explanation of a knowledge worker's productivity. He explains 'knowledge work' as:

> The first requirement in tackling knowledge work is to find out what the task is so as to make it possible to concentrate knowledge workers on the task and to eliminate everything else—at least as far as it can possibly be eliminated. This requires that the knowledge workers themselves define what the task is or should be—and only the knowledge workers themselves can do that.
>
> (Drucker, 1999, p. 85)

This begs the question as to who were Drucker's knowledge workers. One answer may be the "technologists" who apply knowledge of the highest order and perform both knowledge work and manual work. Examples include *inter alia*: health-care workers, lab-technicians, rehabilitation technicians, technicians in imaging, dentists, dental-support people, and automobile mechanics (Drucker, 1999). Indeed, the profession of surgeons epitomizes his notion of technologists and he describes their work as follows:

> Surgeons preparing for an operation to correct a brain aneurysm before it produces a lethal brain haemorrhage, spend hours in diagnosis *before* they cut—and that requires specialised knowledge of the highest order. Again, during the surgery, an unexpected complication may occur which calls for theoretical knowledge and judgement, both of the very highest order. However, the surgery itself is manual work—and manual work consisting of repetitive, manual operations in which the emphasis is on speed, accuracy, and uniformity.
>
> (Drucker, 1999, p. 88)

Drucker was influential as a management guru, but his writings are significant in relation to this investigation because he made a major contribution to the debate on knowledge work. He recognized and explicitly acknowledged a new way of working and in doing so he coined the phrase 'knowledge work.' He also introduced a new category of knowledge work, which he termed 'the technologists.' His best example of a technologist or a knowledge worker was a surgeon. He explained that the main function of a surgeon was to diagnose the patient's suitability and requirements for the operation and to perform a successful operation in order to improve the quality of her/his patient's life. In that sense, the nature of work in this technologist's job could not be argued as distinctive or new or different from work carried out by a surgeon in the old economy. However, what may be viewed as new is the use of technologies (and by his use of the new type of working 'technologists'). This reliance on technologies alongside the normal or previous way of working may be connected with views by Bell (1973) and Castells (2000), presented and discussed in the last chapter, where ICET played an important role in the knowledge economy.

The type of knowledge identified in this type of knowledge work as exemplified by a surgeon includes a high degree of specialized and theoretical knowledge. A surgeon's theoretical knowledge is applied before an operation to ascertain the nature of the operation and during the operation to adjust and adapt to the realities of the situation. This theoretical knowledge is similar to Bell's (1973) version in terms of discipline-related knowledge but different in that Drucker (1999) does not include an element of research and development whereas Bell does.

In order to carry out this type of knowledge work, a worker needs to draw on certain specific skills and abilities, and supporting activities such as past professional experiences and additional training. In the case of Drucker's surgeon, professional judgement as well as high levels of precision, speed, and repetitive action supported by specialized and theoretical knowledge, 'technological skills,' are required. These technological skills are learnt during the surgeon's training and on qualification, the surgeon undergoes continuous professional development. Technological skills are developed during and after qualification through professional practice.

Drucker's technologists were similar to those identified by Bell and Castells. The workers apply their knowledge (echoing versions of "theoretical knowledge" by Bell (1973), Drucker (1999) and Castell's (2000) digitalized version of science-related ideas) as individuals using ICET in incremental stages to improve processes or products. However, the three writers mentioned here refer to traditional sectors and did not discuss new ones. One possible reason for this is the possible lack of evidence of new and emerging sectors such as digital games at the time of their investigations.

Intellective Skills and Training

There are other approaches to knowledge working in addition to the 'technologist' workers. Different skills and abilities are required for working in business organizations and supportive structures such as training opportunities are necessary.

Zuboff (1988), a management sociologist, saw this transformation by IT as having two 'capacities': "automate and informate." She explained the two capacities this way:

> The distinction between *automate* and *informate* provides one way to understand how this technology represents both continuities and discontinuities with the traditions of industrial history. As long as the technology is treated narrowly in its automating function, it perpetuates the logic of the industrial machine that, over the course of this century, has made it possible to rationalize work while decreasing the dependence on human skills. However, the technology also informates the processes to which it is applied, it increases the explicit information content of tasks and sets into motion a series of dynamics that will ultimately reconfigure the nature of work and the social relationships that organise production activity.
>
> (Zuboff, 1988, pp. 10–11)

Automation is necessary in order that "informated workers" (Zuboff, 1988) can use information from automated processes to build and reconfigure products. The informated worker needed to have an "extremely flexible personality" (Zuboff, 2004, p. 323), the ability to exercise critical judgement and work with abstract concepts because the work depended on understanding and manipulating information. Zuboff (1988) also predicted the informated worker would be involved in more intricate work and participate in collaborative teams bound by mutual responsibilities of colleagues.

The cognitive skills and abilities required for this type of work are explained as follows:

> The shifting grounds of knowledge invite managers to recognise the emergent demands for intellective skills and develop a learning environment to which such skills can develop.
>
> (Zuboff, 2004, p. 316)

These skills are:

> Intellective skill is brought to bear in the definition of the problem of analysis, the determination of the data that is required for analysis, the consideration of the appropriateness of an analytical approach, and the application of the analysis to improved performance.
>
> (Zuboff, 2004, p. 320)

Zuboff distinguished the skills required by a machine operator in a paper mill as action-centred and those by an informated operator in the same industry as intellective or cognitive. This difference was articulated by operators in a paper mill in this way:

> With the computer controlling the process, it has cut out the manual labor. You don't have to work hard; you don't have to be out there in the hot, smelly, dirty environment. But it also means that your mind is working twice as hard. Production has increased by about 40 percent. More is being processed and much more quickly. There is a greater flow of data, and so you have to be continuously monitoring and paying attention in order to stay on top of it.
>
> (Zuboff, 1988, pp. 188–189)

Her (Zuboff, 1988, p. 317) assertion was that the knowledge associated with "action-centred skills" (usually related to manual work) was largely tacit in terms of learning/acquisition and execution/performance. The knowledge associated with intellective skills (usually related to mental work) was explicit in the learning or acquisition stage. It was only when the operator became expert in this knowledge that the knowledge could be partly tacit but still largely explicit in the main. She explains the relationship between intellective skills and tacit knowledge as follows:

> intellective mastery will depend upon being able to develop a tacit knowledge that facilitates the recognition of decision alternatives and frees the mind for the kind of insight that could result in innovation and improvement. Such tacit recognition depends upon first being able to explicitly construct the significance of patterns and relationships in the data. Such meanings cannot be achieved without a level of intellective skill development that allows the worker to solve the problem of reference, engage in reasoning that is both inductive and deductive, and apply a conceptual framework to the information at hand. Meaning must be constructed explicitly in order to become implicit later. Intellective skill is necessary for the creation of meaning, and real mastery begins to emerge when such meanings are consolidated in tacit knowledge.
>
> (Zuboff, 1988, pp. 192–193)

What Zuboff meant was that intellective skills were needed to construct patterns and relationships in the IT data. For such skills and abilities to be applied in a business organization, training was necessary whilst on the job (unlike Drucker's technologist training which is after qualification). This development of 'construction' would enable the informated operator to solve the problem of reference, to reason deductively and inductively, and to apply a conceptual framework to the data available (Zuboff, 2004). Having constructed these meanings using intellective skills, the knowledge then become tacit.

Furthermore, there is a perceived outcome to the application of skills and abilities of an 'informate' worker working. It is the ability to recognize that there are appropriate decision options and this would enable and allow him/her (the operator) to use his/her ingenuity to innovate and improve on current processes. These possible innovative practices are a form of creativity and will be explored further in the next chapter. Zuboff (2004) views the interface of workers applying their intellective skills and the organizations or learning environments as:

> The informated workplace, which may no longer be a 'place' at all, is an arena through which information circulates, information to which intellective effort is applied. The quality, rather than the quantity, of effort will be the source from which added value is derived.
>
> (Zuboff, 2004, p. 318)

Zuboff viewed this added value as coming from the quality of application of intellective skills by informated workers which could bring about innovative practices as indicated above.

This research argues for a different approach to knowledge work on the basis that knowledge work occurs at a more analytical level because decisions are made by informated workers. They are dependent upon their own individual understanding of data and training. The prerequisite to this is that workers have to understand the concepts underpinning the data, which a) assists them to define the problems, b) determine the appropriate data for analysis, and c) allows them to choose and apply the option to find solutions (e.g., to improve productivity). However, knowledge workers do not always engage in this process explicitly. Instead, they unconsciously draw on their "sapient tacit knowledge" (Guile, 2006, p. 362) of theoretical and practical knowhow. In this type of process, any ensuing improvements or innovations can be arguably described as a form of creativity (albeit of a problem-solving variety).

Turning to the connections with writers mentioned in the previous chapter, Nonaka and Takeuchi (1995) and Zuboff (2004) refer to workers in business organizations. Zuboff's informated operator relies on her/his past work experiences to assist her/him to relate to abstracted IT data to identify the best possible option to improve processes. This use of previous work experiences has similarities with Nonaka and Takeuchi's knowledge workers where they use previous work experiences as tacit knowledge for innovative knowledge creation. However, the use of past work experiences is different in the two cases. Zuboff's workers use tacit knowledge cognitively and independently. Nonaka and Takeuchi's workers use past work knowledge collaboratively and in social activities making it more tacit. Zuboff's version is more related to the individual type of Polanyi's (1966), whereas Nonaka and Takeuchi's (1995) is more social.

Cross-Disciplinary and Collaborative Working

Following from the above, this section makes a case for another form of knowledge work, which is more collaborative and occurs in social-cultural environments of business organizations. The knowledge, skills, and abilities necessary for it are different to the previous ones and a supportive organizational structure is necessary for its pursuit.

This approach to knowledge work is explained by Nonaka and Takeuchi (1995) in their 'middle-up-down' management model. Their 'Knowledge-Creating Crew' comprises of knowledge practitioners, knowledge engineers, and knowledge officers. The central emphasis of innovative Japanese companies is the heavy use of:

> two-way communications such as dialogue, camp sessions, and drinking sessions (in fact, some companies use the word "nommunication," which is a hybrid created by combining a Japanese word for drinking, "nomu," with "communication," to describe this kind of session) and make frequent use of metaphors and analogies.
>
> (Nonaka and Takeuchi, 1995, p. 151)

This system includes employees from a three-tier management hierarchy namely: front-line employees and line managers as knowledge practitioners; middle managers as knowledge engineers; and top managers as knowledge officers. Each type of knowledge worker requires different forms of knowledge, skills, abilities, and experiences.

Knowledge practitioners (Nonaka and Takeuchi, 1995) are of two types: a) knowledge operators and b) knowledge specialists, who are at the front line of a business organization where they accumulate, generate, and update tacit and explicit knowledge. This group uses both manual (or action-centred skills) and cognitive skills and tacit and explicit knowledge. This is in contrast to Zuboff's (2004) informated operators who have moved away from manual work to informated work requiring mainly cognitive skills, which she calls "intellective skills."

Knowledge specialists perform different functions from operators. Nonaka and Takeuchi perceive the knowledge practitioners as having the following credentials:

> (1) they need to have high intellectual standards; (2) they need to have a strong sense of commitment to re-create the world according to their own perspective; (3) they need to have a wide variety of experiences, both insides and outside the company; (4) they need to be skilled in carrying on a dialogue with customers as well as with colleagues within the company; and (5) they need to be open to carrying out candid discussions as well as debates with others.
>
> (Nonaka and Takeuchi, 1995, p. 153)

Communication skills include debating skills, wide life experiences, and high intellect are specified as qualities for this group of knowledge workers by Nonaka and Takeuchi (1995).

The job of knowledge engineers is to interface with top management, and to re-make reality according to the top management's vision. Nonaka and

Takeuchi (1995) suggested that knowledge engineers re-made reality by converting knowledge through four modes of knowledge conversion especially in the externalization mode of converting tacit images and perspectives into explicit concepts. To do this, knowledge engineers needed to liaise and collaborate with colleagues at different organizational levels to ensure management and coordination. The last of the knowledge crew are the knowledge officers at the senior-most level in the organization. Their principal task includes management of the knowledge-creation process through a hands-on approach, which directs and establishes a vision and sets standards for future projects. These capabilities, which have not been mentioned in previous research, relate to leadership qualities such as: laying down a vision, selection of appropriate human resources, and ensuring project compliance with the organization's strategy. In the next chapter on creativity, these qualities of leadership will be investigated further.

An objective assessment of the study reveals the following: Nonaka and Takeuchi (1995) offer four varieties of workers: knowledge operators and knowledge specialists making up knowledge practitioners (who are the front-line workers and line managers), knowledge engineers (who are the middle managers) and knowledge officers (who are the top managers). The hierarchical approach offers a sense of continuity between the industrial economy and the emerging knowledge economy. Indeed, as the previous chapter on the knowledge economy pointed out, the knowledge economy is in a transitional phase and this perspective provides a sociological and business bridge to knowledge working.

All of the knowledge crew are highly educated (with university-related and/or equivalent qualifications) and are highly skilled workers. Their knowledge is both tacit and explicit with four modes of knowledge conversion.

The second point relates to knowledge creation in organizations and management agendas. The knowledge creation approach as offered by Nonaka and Takeuchi (1995) is a process-driven management, which is 'middle-up-down-management.' It involves team working where individuals are seen as a resource. These authors argued that the Japanese cultural dimension was an important factor in this management style. The investigative areas opened by Nonaka and Takeuchi for this research are useful as they encompass a variety of different areas in organization and human resource management, culture, and teamwork for knowledge creation.

The characteristics of the process described by Nonaka and Takeuchi have connections with Knorr Cetina (2001b, p. 186) who used "lateral and angular branching off of strands of practice" to describe the possibilities of creative divergences and continuation of practices in epistemic cultures. Nonaka and Takeuchi's creation of knowledge required an organization to have a type of epistemic culture with a social and cultural dimension. This was so that workers with different tacit knowledge (work experiences, perceptions, and opinions), explicit knowledge (discipline knowledge), skills, and abilities could work towards a commercial goal strategically and effectively. In Knorr

Cetina's epistemic culture, there is the implication of a social setting such as high-energy physics but without the explicit nature of working with others with different knowledge types. Knorr Cetina's notion of epistemic culture is discipline-related with little emphasis of knowledge types, unlike Nonaka and Takeuchi. In Nonaka and Takeuchi's case, it is at an organizational level with cross-disciplinary or more than one discipline-related field of explicit and tacit knowledge in a collaborative setting.

Creative Personalities and Aesthetic Sensibilities

The section argues that skills and abilities, personalities, and creativity of workers are important in the eventual production of commercial goods.

In the previous three types of knowledge work, skills and abilities were relevant to knowledge work. This section makes a case for the inclusion of personalities and their creativity. Reich's (2001, p. 48) "creative workers" were:

> At the core of innovation lie two distinct personalities representing different inclinations, talents, and ways of perceiving the world.
>
> (Reich, 2001, p. 49)

His two distinct personalities of creative workers are geeks and shrinks. A "geek" is:

> The artist or inventor, the designer, the engineer, the financial wizard, the geek, the scientist, the writer or musician—the person who, in short, is capable of seeing new possibilities in a particular medium and who takes delight in exploring and developing them.
>
> (Reich, 2001, p. 49)

A geek has an all-consuming passion to create new possibilities. She/he is not antisocial but empathy is not her/his forte. She/he is happier interacting with technology or another medium or with a group of people collaborating in achieving something 'ultra cool.'

Reich's other creative personality is the shrink whose strength is not interacting with technology but with people. Her/his skills are:

> That of the marketer, the talent agent, the rainmaker, the trend spotter, the producer, the consultant, the hustler—the person, in short, who can identify possibilities in the marketplace for what other people might want to have, see, or experience, and who understands how to deliver on these opportunities.
>
> (Reich, 2001, p. 51)

Reich equates these two creative workers with job personalities by adopting a cognitive psychological approach. This form of knowledge work involving creativity has opened up a new area for understanding work in the knowledge economy, which will be discussed in the next chapter and in the four empirical chapters on advertising and IT software (Chapters 6 to 9).

The other characteristic of these creative workers is the possibility of closer interactions with end users as exemplified by Quah (2002) in the previous chapter. Reich uses an example of a shrink—the architect Thierry Despont—to illustrate this characteristic:

> To be successful at my job," he says, "one must be very good at under-standing the client's needs but also the client's dreams and memories. One must know where the client comes from and what they desire. Part of the craft of learning to read people, to see things they are sure about, the things they are unsure about; the things they don't convey verbally, but express through their surroundings.
>
> (Reich, 2001, p. 53)

Reich's writings are particularly significant in relation to this research because he replaced the centrality of knowledge in knowledge work with the idea of creativity, by-passing the difficulty of using knowledge and having to define it in writing about knowledge work. Having said that, Reich implied that cre-ative workers had the ability to seek out and solve problems and to manipulate symbols but these were reliant on them having acquired a body of previous knowledge. This knowledge consisted of a high level of formal education to first degree and beyond, informal education, and learning and interacting at work. These sociological factors together with the creative workers' entrepre-neurial abilities enabled them to commercially exploit new possibilities and gave them a link to creativity and knowledge work. It is this explicit con-nection with creativity that makes Reich's approach to knowledge working distinctive to the previous three writers discussed, i.e., Drucker (1993), Nonaka and Takeuchi (1995) and Zuboff (2004).

Reich's research on creative workers connects with Lash and Urry's (1994) from the previous chapter. The difference is in the naming of settings: Reich (2001) uses "media" (such as software, entertainment and music) and Lash and Urry (1994) use "culture industries." An important point of connection refers to notions of creativity. Reich (2001) uses creative personalities and insights to describe how workers add value to the knowledge economy. Lash and Urry (1994) describe how those in the culture industries add value to a product through branding using their aesthetic sensibilities, which are semiotic skills and abilities.

However, despite these contributions, two areas of importance have been underplayed by Reich. The first relates to Reich's use of anecdotal rather than empirical evidence. This need for empirical evidence to secure academic cred-ibility has created a research space for this investigation. However, his writing provides this investigation with a direction to some areas of knowledge work previously not researched. The second area is the nature of the tasks carried out in a 'role.' A role is used instead of a profession or an occupation in order to denote the work changes in the knowledge economy. He glossed over the functions that are found in a role/job, for instance, how they fitted into a real-life sector like computer software (due to the lack of empirical evidence). This begs the question: did he imply that the people working in different jobs conformed to the work patterns of either a geek or a shrink? This generic view provides this book the opportunity to investigate the micro-level nature of different roles in a sector of the knowledge economy, i.e., the intra-sectoral-dimension, and over different sectors, i.e., the inter-sectoral-dimension.

Some Issues and Perspectives of Knowledge Work

This final section provides a definition of knowledge for the purposes of this research and a summary of the four approaches of knowledge work, based on the literature reviews from this and previous chapters. This summary provides a platform to link knowledge work with creativity and leads into the next chapter.

Knowledge is defined eclectically here to include discipline-related knowledge from sciences, technology, or culture industries and cross-disciplinary knowledge, e.g., collaborative applications of knowledge. It can be codified, digitalized, or transmitted through the Internet. It may be tacit in nature and it is used independently or collaboratively to improve a process/product, find a solution to a problem, or as a resource for product development. This approach to the definition of knowledge is justified on the basis that it brings together insights from different scholars.

Moving to the investigation of this chapter, knowledge work may be defined as the application of knowledge for commercial ends. It uses technologies (e.g., computer software and the Internet) and technological objects (e.g., laptop, netbook, and mobile phone). Application of knowledge or knowledge work is a conscious activity to create or improve a commercial product or a service. Knowledge work may also occur in the form of improving an existing process by deciding on the best available option. These applications may be carried independently or collaboratively or in a variation of both.

This chapter argued that there was no one approach to knowledge working as the new economy was in transition. Four types of workers: 'technologists,' 'informated' workers, 'knowledge-creating crew,' and 'creative workers' were investigated. Three main overarching themes were identified. The first was skills, abilities, and personalities were needed for workers to invent or discover new possibilities or what was needed in terms of new products or services. The second was workers who use their education, training, and work experiences to ascertain the best available options to improve work processes. This training involved understanding abstracted data generated by information technology systems. The training may be ongoing even after a worker has qualified professionally as continuous professional development. The third related to collaborative work approaches and organizational settings of knowledge working.

This involved educated and skilled participants with skills and attributes collaborating to create innovative products and/or services.

However, all the four knowledge work approaches were investigated at a generic level—i.e., the types of knowledge work were applicable to the new economy and did not offer specific roles/jobs. They might not be applicable to specific roles/jobs in the advertising and IT software sector nor to roles between sectors. This research aims to understand the complexity of knowledge work at intra and inter-sectoral levels.

As mentioned at the start, the knowledge economy is in transition and, consequently, a more relational approach to viewing work is necessary. This is where the innovation of this investigation lies. Despite the diversity of knowledge work examined in this chapter, there is a common thread, which runs through the approaches of knowledge work and this is the creative use of knowledge to produce innovative knowledge goods. The creative dimensions in terms of knowledge work will be examined further in the next chapter.

4 Critical Perceptions of Creativity and Knowledge Work

Introduction

This chapter relates to the fourth research question and focuses on descriptions of creativity important to knowledge work. It argues there is no one view of creativity for knowledge work and it requires specific skills, abilities, and personalities. It notes that creative workers require ongoing support and creative work may be collaborative and/or independent.

Descriptions of Creativity in Relation to Knowledge Work

This section focuses on four descriptions of creativity in relation to knowledge work. Gardner (1984) provides an individual perspective whilst the other three writers offer social perspectives of creativity. Csikszentmihalyi (1988) explains it as a systems process where creativity occurs in a socio-cultural environment. Sternberg et al. (2004) study creative leadership variety in collaborative settings, and von Hippel (2006) provides a digital understanding of creative working where users and producers create collaboratively. The rationale for relying on these descriptions of creativity in relation to knowledge work is to provide a greater understanding of it, rather than carry out a comprehensive review of all scholarly articles in this area.

Individual, Intelligence, and Enculturation

This section argues that individuals, using their skills and abilities, apply creativity to their commercial activities and they require supportive frameworks for its application. Workers use their skills and abilities in knowledge work in a creative manner. One approach of how these are utilized is by Gardner (1999). He explains his notion of intelligences as follows:

> After all, intelligences arise from the combination of a person's genetic heritage and life conditions in a given culture and era.
>
> (Gardner, 1999, p. 45)

The mention of culture is critical because it echoes the possible work conditions that may be necessary for the production of goods or services. These intelligences are described as discrete intelligences. He acknowledged the notion of a multiplicity of intelligences as:

> the conviction that there exist at least some intelligences, that these are relatively independent of one another, and that they can be fashioned and combined in a multiplicity of adaptive ways by individuals and cultures, seems to me to be increasingly difficult to deny.
>
> (Gardner, 1993, pp. 8–9)

He based his argument for the concept of multiple intelligences (MI) on various sources of evidence.[1] The descriptions of these intelligences are important here because they provide a way of defining and typologizing intelligence, which may be linked to genetic and socio-cultural environments and creativity. These seven intelligences are: linguistic (capacity to learn and apply languages for certain aims), logical-mathematical (ability to analyze problems, apply mathematics in a scientific manner), musical (ability to perform, compose, and appreciate musical patterns), bodily-kinesthetic (capability of using one's body towards fashioning goods and solving problems), spatial (ability to recognize and manipulate patterns of spaces for a purpose), interpersonal (capability to understand others and use it to work effectively with them) and intrapersonal (ability to understand oneself and use it to regulate one's life effectively) (the last two are known collectively as personal), and naturalist intelligence (ability to recognize and classify the flora and fauna of one's environment) (Gardner, 1999).

Every individual has a "unique blend of intelligences" (Gardner, 1999, p. 45) which are a 'combination of genetic heritage and life conditions.' In terms of supportive structures, Gardner would most likely include: parental support (cultural, sporting, and related activities that provide an experience of the world); academic qualifications (in-depth knowledge of subject areas used in knowledge work); and life experiences (popular cultural that may be used in the workplace). These inputs are a useful platform of work for a creative worker. What is unclear is the relationship between the genetic inheritance and life conditions. However, in his revised edition "Frames of Mind," Gardner (1993) acknowledged a 'shift in philosophy of assessment' in which he made the distinction between "intelligences, domains, and fields"[2] that led to his notion of creativity.

Creativity in relation to these abilities and skills or multiple intelligences is described as a three-dimensional taxonomy. According to Gardner (1993, pp. xx–xxi), the 'individual' used his/her intelligence, which was formed at birth. The individual is brought up in socio-cultural environments consisting of different 'domains' (Gardner, 1993, pp. xx–xxi), which consisted of "disciplines or crafts" by which the person was "encultured" in the process of "socialization" through the application of more than one type of intelligence.

In this way the individual achieved a degree of expertise. For instance, a musician with a musical intelligence, according to Gardner (1993), was insufficient to be competent. He/she needed other types of intelligences by which they were "encultured and socialized" through and in an environment. The individual's degree of expertise was judged by experts or institutions, which Gardner (1993, pp. xx–xxi) called 'field.' The implication was that a facilitative social environment was required for the development of a relevant set of intelligences to become competent, and genetic factors alone were insufficient.

He defined a creative person as one:

> who *regularly* solves problems or fashions products in a *domain*, and whose work is considered both novel and acceptable by knowledgeable members of a field.
>
> (Gardner, 1993, p. xxi)

Gardner (1999, pp. 116–117) made a distinction between "intelligences" and "creativity." According to him, the realization of a person's creativity occurred by the intricate interactions of intelligences, domains, and fields where life conditions were an important factor. A creative person needed to ask new questions over and above those questions asked by an intelligent person. A creative person sought novelty, or a new angle when reviewing a situation and operated in a domain or discipline which could result in the creation of a timely new idea or product that was acknowledged by experts in that field.

Having examined the 'individual'-centred approaches to creativity, the following sections examine three social and collaborative forms of creativity, the first being collaborative creative working.

A Socio-Cultural Approach to Creativity

This section notes another form of creative work, which involves collaboration in a socio-cultural environment. It requires supportive structures so that workers may perform their commercial activities effectively. Creative work involves more than just individuals working independently and includes a wider social system which is explained by Csikszentmihalyi as:

> what we call creative is never the result of individual action alone; it is the product of three main shaping forces: a set of social institutions, or *field*, that selects from the variations produced by individuals those that are worth preserving; a stable cultural *domain* that will preserve and transmit the selected new ideas or forms to the following generations; and finally the *individual*, who brings about some change in the domain, a change that the field will consider to be creative.
>
> (Csikszentmihalyi, 1988, p. 325)

What he meant was that a creative individual could not work entirely independently but was shaped by the work environment or organization and also by the area (e.g., advertising) of the work. He explained the relationship between creativity and the 'socio-cultural system' as follows:

> Creativity is a phenomenon that results from interaction between these three systems. Without a culturally defined domain of action in which innovation is possible, the person cannot even get started. And without a group of peers to evaluate and confirm the adaptiveness of the innovation, it is impossible to differentiate what is creative from what is simply statistically improbable or bizarre.
>
> (Csikszentmihalyi, 1988, p. 326)

From this it may be concluded that an individual could not be creative without the existence of a domain where the creative action was transmitted and without a field where others acknowledged the creativity. This is an important idea for this investigation because it suggests that there is a clear relationship between a knowledge worker's creative activities and the wider socio-cultural environment.

Indeed his notion of "collaboration" consisted of more than just a group of individuals coming together for a project with a defined outcome. There was also necessity for a "culture" where the required knowledge for creativity had to be made available to those who wanted to use it. The two words: collaboration and culture are connected with the concepts propounded by Nonaka and Takeuchi (1995), who examined knowledge work and the communication systems used by members working collaboratively. These members used their explicit and tacit knowledge (of experiences and perceptions) for innovating products. These scholars firmly believed that to be effective, business organizations needed to function in a social-cultural environment and also needed a culture for such activities to occur.

Csikszentmihalyi (1988, p. 330) explained an individual's creative act by its very definition was different and novel from the idea of the existing ideas in a domain, and he called this a "variation." This 'variation' comes from two sources, from the person's inheritance or genetic make-up, and from life experiences. Genetic make-up was culturally defined and a "product of three main shaping forces" (Csikszentmihalyi, 1988, p. 325), which comprised of a) field, b) domain, and c) the person. Thus, genetic inheritance on its own without the social interactions did not create a variation.

Further forms of creativity are highlighted by these examples: 'learned cognitive flexibility,' 'a more dogged motivation,' and 'rare event in life' are equally important in producing variations. Examples of supportive structures in terms of 'learned cognitive flexibility' (Csikszentmihalyi, 1988, p. 330) include: a supportive home environment where a person can experiment without worry of conformity or failure and re-training at work or at a higher education institution which enables the person to extend his/her analytical talents. A person's motivation may be a result of a combination of 'inheritance' and personal experiences. A 'rare event in life' could be in the form of meeting someone who might change his/her life significantly such as providing him/her with the confidence to work in a certain domain or allowing him/her to alter his attitude to life (Csikszentmihalyi, 1988, p. 330).

Time is also a relevant factor as it adds another layer of complexity to creative working where there needs a period of gestation to work through from one system to another (Csikszentmihalyi, 1988). Part of this process involves comparison, evaluation, and interpretation where gatekeepers engage with an innovative idea. This form of engagement requires active communication between the creator and other collaborators. This 'collaboration' is not the traditional notion of 'collaboration' but it nevertheless implies a wider notion of networking between various parties and the creator to achieve a recognizable outcome (in the form of acknowledgement of the outcome as innovative).

The other point relates to the impact of technology (Csikszentmihalyi, 1988) as the time span for an innovative idea/outcome to be acknowledged and appreciated is often quite short in the knowledge economy.

Creative Leadership Practices

This section offers another form of creativity away from an individual or collaborative perspective and is focused on leadership in a commercial environment. This form of creativity also requires skills and abilities, which are appropriate to an organization at a specific commercial state.

A form of creativity that is related to leadership environments is suggested by Sternberg et al. (2004) in their 'Propulsion Model of Creative Leadership' which saw leadership not only in terms of creativity but also in all fields including the arts, the humanities, and the sciences. Furthermore, Sternberg et al. examine leadership in business and organizations, which is in tandem with the commercial dimension of the study. This investigation will argue that this commercial criterion has strong similarities with the previous notion of creative process because of a common financial criterion.

Sternberg et al. (2004) used the notion of "propulsion" as a metaphor in the context of the types of leadership where a leader aimed to lead from a starting point of where the organization was and to the future. In this model (Sternberg et al., 2004), there are three kinds of creative leadership: namely, those that accept current paradigms and attempt to extend them, those that reject current paradigms and attempt to replace them, and those that integrate existing paradigms to create a new one. In total, there are eight ways of exerting creative leadership (Sternberg et al., 2004).

The first kind is where the leaders accept current paradigms/assumptions and apply them in new ways. Sternberg et al. describe these leaders:

> Thus they do not defy the crowd, but rather, 'move' it to a new location. They are most likely to be found in organizations that have strong cultures

that they do not wish to change, or that view themselves as succeeding the way they are and hence are reluctant to tamper with what they view as a winning strategy.

(Sternberg et al., 2004, p. 146)

In this kind of creative leadership, there are four types; replication, redefinition, forward incrementation, and advance forward incrementation. A "replicative leader" wants to maintain the status quo of the organization (Sternberg et al., 2004, p. 146). She/he is appointed when the organization is successful and the job of the leader is to make sure it stays on its present course.

With the "redefinition leadership", Sternberg et al. say:

This type of leadership is an attempt to show that a field or organization is in the right place, but not for the reason(s) that others, including previous leaders, think it is. The current status of the organization thus is seen from a different point of view. The propulsion leads to circular motion, such that the creative leadership directs back to where the organization is, but as viewed in a different way.

(Sternberg et al., 2004, p. 147)

An example of this type of creative leadership can be seen in the use of aspirin, a pain relief drug (Sternberg et al., 2004, p. 147). The manufacturer's clever redefinition and repositioning of the drug has ensured that aspirin is now also commonly used as a blood thinner to prevent heart attacks.

In defining "forward incrementation leadership" they say it is where:

one takes on the helm with the idea of advancing the leadership programme of whomever one has succeeded. The promise is of progress through continuity. Creativity through forward incrementation is probably the kind that is most easily recognised and appreciated as creativity.

(Sternberg et al., 2004, p. 148)

This leadership style focuses on incremental and innovative products such as Honda cars (an example also used by Nonaka and Takeuchi, 1995).

The last type is the "advance forward incrementation leadership" which moves beyond the ordinary to venture out even further. The propulsive force is one of forward motion albeit accelerated beyond the confines of perceptions.

Having discussed the acceptance of the current vision, which is inherited and the four approaches one can do to change it as examined by Sternberg et al. (2004), it is useful to point out that in the context of study, this typology of leadership styles enables this study to identify and examine in greater detail the possible forms of leadership styles in the two empirical chapters.

The next kind of creative leadership includes the rejection of current paradigms and replacement of them. There are three types namely: "redirection, reconstruction/redirection and re-initiation" (Sternberg et al., 2004, p. 149).

In "redirective leadership," the leader propels the organization in a different direction to the one previously taken. Examples included binary computers in comparison with calculators, electric cars, and electric razors. They perform the same functions but in a new way (Sternberg et al., 2004, p. 149).

In the case of "reconstruction/redirection," the leader attempts to:

> move a field or an organization or a product line back to where it once was (a reconstruction of the past) so that it may move onward from that point, but in a direction different from the one it took from that point onward.
>
> (Sternberg et al., 2004, p. 149)

The examples include Brill Cream and watches with mechanical movements by manufactures like Rolex (modern versions of old nostalgic products) (Sternberg et al., 2004, p. 149).

With re-initiation leadership, a leader wants to move a field, organization, or product line to a different starting base, that is not yet exploited, and then to move even further from there. In propulsion terms, it is the movement from a new starting point in the direction from that field, organization, or product line.

The last kind of leadership involves "integrating existing paradigms" to create a new one (Sternberg et al., 2004, p. 150). There is only one type which is "synthesis leadership" where the leader:

> integrates two ideas that previously were seen as unrelated or even as opposed. What formerly were viewed as distinct ideas are now viewed as related, and capable of being unified. Integration is a key means by which progress is attained in the sciences.
>
> (Sternberg et al., 2004, p. 150)

The typology of creative leadership styles is also connected to Nonaka and Takeuchi (1995) whose ideas were discussed in the previous chapter. They investigated the ways in which a knowledge officer was a leader who envisioned a strategy to innovate a product in a social-cultural environment. Thus, there are echoes of similarity and resonance in the different ideas.

Technology and the Democratization of Innovation

This section argues for a perspective of creativity where producers and users work collaboratively towards the production of goods mediated by technologies. This form of creativity is researched by von Hippel (2006), and he explains the trend towards "democratization of innovation" (von Hippel, 2006, p. 1) as follows:

> When I say that innovation is being democratized, I mean that users of products and services—both firms and individual consumers—are increasingly able to innovate for themselves. User-centered innovation processes offer great advantages over the manufacturer-centric innovation

development systems that have been the mainstay of commerce for hundreds of years. Users that innovate can develop exactly what they want, rather than relying on manufacturers to act as their (often imperfect) agents.

(von Hippel, 2006, p. 1)

He offers an explanation for the trend in which the growing sophistication and cost reduction of technologies—software and hardware—has a major impact on innovative process. This process affects not only the traditional manufacturer but also the consumer. The consumer is less dependent on the manufacturer in obtaining a product exactly to his specifications and needs. Furthermore, the consumer/user may innovate using readily accessible technologies.

Von Hippel refers to "users" as:

firms or individual consumers that expect to benefit from *using* a product or a service. In contrast, manufacturers expect to benefit from *selling* a product or a service. A firm or an individual can have different relationships to different products or innovations.

(von Hippel, 2006, p. 3)

Some examples of products where there are a significant percentage of developing or modifying products for their own use include: printed circuit CAD software, library information systems, surgical equipment, Apache OS server software security features, outdoor consumer products, 'extreme sporting equipment' (e.g., canyoning which combines mountain climbing, abseiling, and swimming in canyons) and mountain biking equipment (von Hippel, 2006, p. 20).

This notion of 'democratization of innovation' is a development from Quah's (2002) idea of closer collaboration between consumers and producers. This innovation of products or services may be carried out between users and/or with firms.

Implications for the Investigation Based on the Four Reviews

This chapter argued that there were four perspectives of creativity in connection with knowledge work. These included: a) individuals who worked independently or b) in collaboration, c) workers who took a leadership role, and d) those who were producers and collaborated with consumers using technologies to produce innovative products. From these forms of creativity in knowledge work, two themes emerged. The first related to the application of cognitive abilities (e.g., skills, talents, and personalities) in creative knowledge work, and the second, the types and degrees of enculturation in order that creative work might be performed.

The literature on creativity in the context of knowledge working investigated above has varying perspectives as it is drawn from a variety of disciplines. Chapter 10 will put forward a relational approach to provide insights into creative knowledge working.

Notes

1. There are critics to Gardner's sources of evidence for the lack of statistical data. They include K. Richardson (1991), F. Smolucha (1993) and L. Waterhouse (2006). J. White (1998) was critical regarding the use of the eight criteria.
2. Gardner acknowledged the taxonomy of intelligences, domains, and fields to the research work done by D. Feldman (1980), D. Feldman and L. Goldsmith (1986) and M. Csikszentmihalyi (1988).

5   A Theoretical Framework of Creative Knowledge Work

Introduction

This chapter presents the final stages in the development of a distinct theoretical framework to investigate creative knowledge work and workers, drawing on the previous three theoretical chapters and an interdisciplinary and relational approach.

Knowledge Work Themes

Three major themes relating to knowledge work were identified in Chapter 3. The first related to an individualist manner of working where workers applied their cognitive abilities and creative personalities in the areas of science, technology, or culture industries to invent or discover new possibilities—e.g., a medium, product, or service. The second theme noted that workers through the application of their education and training (possibly postqualification and related to an understanding of abstracted data generated by information technology systems) and work experiences, determined what was the best option available to them to improve work processes. The third theme was concerned with the need for collaboration by creative workers and investigated organizational settings where knowledge work occurred. Collaborative creative work, it was noted, involved both highly educated and skilled participants with a variety of different skills and attributes, who collaborated as a team and shared and used their collective knowledge to create innovative products and/ or services.

Creativity Themes

In the previous chapter, two prominent themes emerged: a) workers and their skills, abilities, and attributes involved in creative knowledge work, and b) the types and degrees of enculturation. The first theme related to workers who use their skills and talents in varying degrees in a collaborative work context and this was accentuated by the relationship between genetic heritage and sociocultural environments. The second theme identified was "enculturation"

(Gardner, 1993, p. xx), of which two main approaches were distilled: a) a supportive ICET environment was critical particularly where artefacts (e.g., software programmes) had a crucial role to play in supporting the creation of innovative goods/services, and b) positive life conditions/experiences such as a supportive home and work environments as well as a facilitative academic work contexts (e.g., with accessibility to current social knowledge) enabled creative work to be produced and acknowledged.

Connections between the Themes

The themes from the Chapter 3 on knowledge work and Chapter 4 on creativity are discussed below to emphasize the connections in terms of similarities and differences between writers. These connections will lead on to the development of a conceptual framework of creative knowledge work in this chapter.

The first connection refers to supportive environments that facilitate the enculturation of workers into established and/or new routines and workplace practices (Gardner, 1993, pp. xx–xxi). These supportive environments relate to education, training and work, and life experiences. The key issues that arose from Chapter 3 were: the value of training after highly educated technologists are qualified (Drucker, 1993); the value of re-training to informated workers (Zuboff, 1988); the critical importance of providing a supportive and constructive work environment where tacit knowledge (gleaned from work experiences and perspectives) can be shared to facilitate innovative activities (Nonaka and Takeuchi, 1995); and the significance of providing a supportive home environment to facilitate creative activities (Reich, 2001).

Turning to Chapter 4, the creative activities of knowledge workers reflected the following perspectives, which ranged from: the necessity for a unique combination of intelligences (Gardner, 1993, pp. xx–xxi), the identification of supportive life experiences such as "learned cognitive flexibility, motivation and rare event in life," the notion that failing is not a negative but rather a learning experience, conformity was not always necessary, the confidence and courage to pursue ideas/activities was very important, as was the self-belief that one could alter one's attitude to life (Csikszentmihalyi's, 1988, p. 330). In addition, workers required a supportive working digital environment, which was created through assistance from their fellow collaborators in the creation of innovations goods/services (von Hippel, 2006).

The new perspectives that emerged from writers discussed in Chapter 4, included: the interaction of supportive life conditions/socio-cultural environments together with genetic heritage so that creative knowledge work can be carried out (Csikszentmihalyi, 1988; Gardner, 1993); and the importance of a supportive ICET environment (e.g., where artefacts such as software programmes play an important role) in the innovation of products and services (von Hippel, 2006).

The other identifiable connection between the themes of knowledge work and creativity related to workers' application of their cognitive skills, talents, and personalities, which are used individually (Chapter 3, Zuboff, 1988; Drucker, 1999; Reich, 2001 and in Chapter 4, Gardner, 1999; von Hippel, 2006) or collaboratively (Chapter 3, Nonaka and Takeuchi, 1995 and in Chapter 4, Csikszentmihalyi, 1988; Sternberg et al., 2004; von Hippel, 2006).

The individuals who applied their cognitive abilities in their work activities differed in styles: the technologists used theoretical knowledge to implement their work with the assistance of technologies (Drucker, 1999); the informated workers applied past work experiences and utilized abstract IT data (Zuboff, 1988) to determine cognitively the best available process option for product development/improvement; and the creative workers used their creative personalities to identify and solve problems in specific media contexts to create innovative products (Reich, 2001). Whilst some creative workers applied their cognitive abilities to ask new questions and seek novelty in the manufacture and development of new ideas/products (Gardner, 1999), other used their cognitive abilities towards the innovation of new products in a digital media platform (e.g., on the Internet) (von Hippel, 2006). Chapter 4 distinguished new perspectives on creativity in the context of cognitive abilities. The first included the posing of new questions and the seeking of novelty (Gardner, 1999, p. 45) through a combination of the workers' "genetic inheritance and life conditions" which occurs via socialization or "enculturation" (Gardner, 1993, pp. xx–xxi). The other perspective related to users/consumers and producers who worked collaboratively towards a new product mediated by advanced technologies (von Hippel, 2006).

In the context of collaborative style of working, which generally occurs in commercial and digital environments, the different aspects include: collaborating during social activities (such as drinking outings), cultural work settings (as in the case of Japanese business organizations) (Nonaka and Takeuchi, 1995), and the combination of a three-dimensional framework of individuals, domain, and field to carry out collaborative work, which can be external to the business organization (Csikszentmihalyi, 1988). In addition, there are leaders who operate in business organizations by persuading, convincing, and motivating workers to execute their vision for the improvement of the financial prospects of their employer companies (Sternberg et al., 2004) and those workers who collaborate via digital media as on the Internet (von Hippel, 2006). In terms of new perspectives from Chapter 4 on creativity in relation to knowledge work, these include: collaborative work covering different settings outside the corporate environment and interactions with experts in their fields (Csikszentmihalyi, 1988); and workers collaborating on a digital dimension where geographical or organizational locations are irrelevant (von Hippel, 2006).

From the psychologists' points of view, the individual style of working (Gardner, 1999) and the collaborative style of working (Csikszentmihalyi, 1988) focus on the relationship between genetic heritage and socio-cultural environments. This nature and nurture debate may be perceived differently where the mind is merely a 'toolkit' and culture "shapes the mind" (Bruner, 1996). This expansive notion of 'culture' may be linked to the discussion of 'context' in relation to knowledge work (in Chapter 3) to invoke the differing social conditions. This expanded relational link is discussed with reference to the definition of "context" (Chaiklin and Lave, 1996) in relation to the primary argument of this study. It was argued that "context" involved sociological forces around temporal dimensions—for instance, work conditions, media types, qualifications, and life experiences. This was connected to a sense of movement between contexts in relation to creative knowledge work (Cole, 1996). The above notions of context may also be applied to the definition of knowledge where relevant knowledge is applied to specific work contexts or where knowledge is re-contextualized to fit the specificity of the work.

In investigating the connections from the themes from Chapter 3 on knowledge work and Chapter 4 on descriptions of creativity and knowledge work, terms such as 'individual' and 'collaborative' styles of work, and 'contexts' were used to describe the similarities and differences in the research of different scholars. These concepts are viewed in relation to each other and the implications of this in relation to the principle question under consideration in this study will be discussed in Chapter 10. The above provides a foundation towards the overall development of the theoretical framework utilized in this research. The framework is examined in the next section with an illustration in Figure 5.1. A summary is provided in the third section.

A Theoretical Framework of Creative Knowledge Work

This section presents a fully developed theoretical framework, drawn from the investigations described in previous chapters. Accordingly, the first part of this section describes the framework as a two-dimensional matrix (Figure 5.1, see below), which features the boundaries of the framework. The horizontal dimension focuses on working styles which include both individually or collaboratively styles of applying knowledge creatively by individuals who utilize their previous experience, relevant skills, abilities, and attributes. The vertical dimension is dependent on context, which can be single or multi-contexts. Context has a more dynamic meaning for the purposes of this investigation, and it includes sociological forces around the nature of working carried out by people such as: temporal dimension; work conditions within and outside an organizational structure; a medium such as a discipline, area, specialism, or sector; using technology; and (academic and non-academic) qualifications and other life experiences that are required for knowledge work. A single context approach refers to people working in one context as described above. A multi-contexts approach may refer to working in or with more than one context, i.e., multi-contexts and/or cross over of more than one context (i.e., inter-contexts).

It may be pointed out that the dimensions are fluid and dynamic and indeed any location on a dimension such as working style is merely an estimation along that spectrum. Located in each of the quadrants of the framework are: a) work approaches (from Chapter 3) and b) descriptions of creativity in relation to work (from Chapter 4). The next part explains each of the quadrants in the framework.

STYLES OF WORKING

CONTEXTS	Individually	Collaboratively
Single	Amplifications of work approaches: Technologists (Drucker, 1993) Informated workers (Zuboff, 1988) Geeks & Shrinks (Reich, 2001) Amplifications of creative descriptions by: Gardner (1999) von Hippel (2006) 1	Amplifications of work approaches: Specialists & Operators (Nonaka & Takeuchi, 1995) Amplifications of creative descriptions by: Csikszentmihalyi (1988) von Hippel (2006) 2
Multi-	Amplifications of work approaches: Technologists (Drucker, 1993) Geeks & Shrinks (Reich, 2001) Amplifications of creative descriptions by: Gardner (1999) von Hippel (2006) 4	Amplifications of work approaches: Engineers & Officers/ Leaders (Nonaka & Takeuchi, 1995) Amplifications of creative descriptions by: Csikszentmihalyi (1988) Sternberg et al. (2004) von Hippel (2006) 3

Figure 5.1 A theoretical framework of creative knowledge work

Description of the Quadrants

The first quadrant from the top left-hand corner (Figure 5.1) indicates an individual working in a single context. The relevant work approaches associated with this quadrant are an 'informated worker.' The informated worker applies intellective skills and draws on job experiences both previous and current, discipline-related knowledge, and a level of understanding of the abstracted data generated by the information technology system of the company. A combination of these together with training is required for the informated worker to make quality decisions with regard to the most appropriate process option.

Another type of knowledge worker: the 'technologist' applies scientific-based knowledge, or theoretical knowledge to knowledge work such as a surgeon who applies theoretical knowledge to study the requirements and operational activities before the operation and then uses hand-operated skills to perform precise and repetitive actions at different speeds to complete tasks. Technologies used before and during the operation assist the surgeon. The acquisition of discipline-based knowledge (in the disciplines of science and technology) and hand-operated skills continue after the acquisition of professional qualifications.

Another group of workers: the 'creative workers' (e.g., 'geeks' and 'shrinks') are those who apply knowledge creatively and have distinct personalities, which facilitate their production of new goods. The former group of workers chooses to explore and develop new possibilities in a medium whereas the latter group anticipates consumers' wants and desires. The geeks' emphasis is on the product while the shrinks' emphasis is on the would-be-customer/user/ consumer. The skills required of creative workers include asking, identifying, solving, and brokering problems either in a particular medium (by the geeks) or with a particular group of people (by the shrinks).

Central to these creative knowledge workers is that they work in a medium (a single context) like IT software in a capacity as a software developer. In order to work creatively, they require different forms of knowledge, which they access through a high level of formal education to degree level (explicit knowledge) and a high level of informal education (tacit knowledge). The knowledge required by these creative knowledge workers is re-contextualized whether through their past experiences and/or advanced technologies in order to meet the specificity of the job. These creative knowledge workers require a combination of supportive and facilitative environments, which are provided by their families, access to learning at work, interactions with work colleagues, and keen awareness of popular culture.

With regard to the creative descriptions of knowledge work that are associated with the first quadrant, there are two. The first relates to a person's realized potential in the form of seven types of intelligences. These multiple intelligences are realized by the 'socialization' process of domain and field where the outcome is given due recognition by experts through features such as advertising. An individual's creative act is viewed in terms of skills and abilities as a result of asking new questions and by solving problems and fashioning products in a single context, like a sector, which is accepted by experts. Examples of these workers may be the geeks and shrinks. Another example may be the informated worker. The choices made by this worker regarding the most efficient processing options available can be said to be innovative.

There is another example of the creative descriptions—opportunities for innovation—in this quadrant with the backdrop of increased access to and cheaper options of technologies such as laptops and Internet facilities. This approach is mediated using technological artefacts in two ways: by finding ways, democratically, to elaborate and extend knowledge, and by combining and creating new products. Indeed, a user may innovate for commercial consumption if he/she finds that there is no product or service in the marketplace that performs according to his/her needs. This opportunity of innovation process marries with the roles of an informated worker, though arguably the two approaches are clearly not identical. While an informated worker uses abstracted data from IT systems and past job experiences in a supportive work environment to decide the best possible operational option, an 'innovative user' applies technology and existing knowhow to create innovative products to fill a missing niche in the market.

The second quadrant relates to collaborative working in a single context. The approaches of knowledge work associated with this quadrant are those by 'operators and specialists' of the 'knowledge-creating crew,' who are highly educated and skilled workers at the front line of a business organization. They accumulate, generate, and update their knowledge. 'Operators' use their technical manuals as well as cognitive skills to provide feedback on determined issues in the workplace. A 'specialist worker' applies explicit knowledge such as codified technical and scientific knowledge and discusses the innovation with people within and outside the company with the aim of solving a common problem.

There are two descriptions of creativity in relation to knowledge work in this quadrant. The first views the creative phenomenon as an interaction between three systems of field (i.e., people who could affect the domain), domain (i.e., a discipline) and individual. The emphasis is on the importance of the 'symbol system of the culture' where a creative act (a change or variation to existing knowledge) is carried out using symbols in a specific domain or discipline. Here the domain is assumed to have the necessary knowledge for a person to understand and apply. The inclusion of symbols may be connected with the aesthetic sensibilities and branding as means of adding value to a product. The creative process must also be acknowledged by the relevant experts in the discipline. This form of interaction requires collaborative actions by the person engaged in or performing the creative act.

Knowledge workers who are involved in the innovative act include 'specialists and operators' who are part of a 'knowledge-creating crew' that has a defined vision to innovate a product.

Like in the previous quadrant, the description of creativity in relation to knowledge work operates against the backdrop of increased access to and more affordable options of technologies, e.g., laptops and Internet facilities. Instead of working independently, the user innovator collaborates with like-minded users to find ways, democratically, to elaborate and extend knowhow/knowledge, and by combining and coming up with new products/services.

As indicated in the first quadrant, there is a degree of fluidity between the quadrants. One possible example of such fluidity may be in the form of a geek who exchanges technical knowledge with similar users via the Internet to try and come up with an improved piece of equipment for a hobby.

The third quadrant relates to collaborative working in multi-contexts. This quadrant sees the work approaches by two members of the knowledge-creating crew: 'engineers and officers.' An engineer would interface with the officer, who as leader provides a vision for a project or for the business organization, and also works with others such as operators and specialists. The engineer has to deal in multi-contexts of knowledge including the different organizational levels in order to convert a vision into reality. The essential skills and abilities include management and coordination of a project to bring about desired outcomes in keeping with the vision. The engineer needs to be highly trained and educated to a high level both academically and professionally together and also needs to be engaged in continuous professional training.

An officer not only has to provide a vision but should also possess skills of persuasion and understand how to use the knowledge and abilities of the team members. He/she needs to be able to rally and motivate them to be part of his/her vision and has the ability to pick the appropriate project leader. Furthermore, he/she requires the tact and diplomacy to be able to interact with others to gain their confidence and respect in order to actualize his/her vision. For an officer or leader, collaboration is an important aspect as well as understanding more than one context of knowledge and interacting in such a way that informs his/her vision. The officer also needs a high level of formal and informal education and training and an empathy with the current work culture in order that he/she can understand and relate to people from differing areas of the organization. He/she should also be able to relate to the external culture and differing contexts such as specialist areas and popular culture to ensure the sustainability of his/her vision.

There are three descriptions of creativity in terms of knowledge work in this quadrant. The essential difference in this quadrant is the multi-contexts dimension. In the case of a social system of field, domain, and individual, a creative person like an engineer (from the knowledge-creating crew) may be working collaboratively in more than one context. In the case of a leader (such as an officer), he/she may envision a project, which traverses several contexts such as mobile phone manufacturing, communication technologies (such as phone, email, radio, and visual screen) and services (such as online gaming and apps). In the case of a group of innovative users, they might create a new piece of equipment for outdoor activities in the canyons, which would consequently incorporate knowledge from several sports like mountain climbing, abseiling, and swimming. Again, as indicated in the second quadrant, the fluidity of other approaches of knowledge work and descriptions of creativity in relation to knowledge work, which may not readily be associated with this quadrant, can occur. A possible example may be a geek (creative worker) who collaborates with other 'innovative users' to produce a new piece of sporting equipment for canyoning.

The final quadrant in Figure 5.1 relates to the individual working in multi-contexts. The work approaches utilized here may be those suggested by 'technologists' or 'geeks' and 'shrinks' as discussed in the first quadrant. A technologist such as a rehabilitation technician may be involved in multiple contexts such as digital simulation of human movement. A geek creative worker for instance may be involved in creating a product such as a tablet computer (e.g., iPad), which requires knowledge of multiple contexts relating to hardware (e.g., connectivity, screen, input, and storage), and software (e.g., audio-visual media). A shrink on the other hand may be involved in ascertaining the needs and wants of people, such as travel information across more than one context such as digital and non-digital media, and travel-related information in areas of geography, leisure, entertainment, travel, accommodation, and politics.

There are two related creative descriptions in this final quadrant: multiple intelligences and closer creative workings between producers and users. The first creative description includes individuals (using their multiple intelligences) who work primarily on their own to create a new product, using their creative skills and talents (and 'encultured' by societal factors), which expand over multiple platforms or contexts. An example of this description may be a shrink working on her/his own and uses her/his intelligences and skills to come up with an idea for a product. An example of such a product is an iPhone, which combines facilities such as phoning, e-mailing, web browsing, searching, and displaying of maps and apps availability. Alongside these capabilities, the product has technologies relating to multi-touch interface and software.[1]

Summary

This chapter explained the development of the theoretical framework of this research. It was informed by the various approaches to knowledge work (from Chapter 3) and the creative descriptions (from Chapter 4). The framework has two dimensions namely: individual and collaborative styles of working, and these operate and are applicable in both single and multi-contexts. Each of the quadrants in the framework was explained in relation to the appropriate approaches of knowledge work and descriptions of creativity in relation to knowledge work.

So far, a generic approach of creative knowledge work based on the theoretical chapters has been investigated. However, this investigation, through the use of empirical data, will offer evidence and discuss in the empirical chapters of 6 to 9 and the final chapter the micro level of creative knowledge application. In particular, the intra- and inter-sectoral creative knowledge work and creative knowledge application, which impact on working cultures/practices, will be investigated.

This study offers an innovative and more nuanced understanding of creative knowledge work and by so doing, answers the research questions on the ways knowledge work is understood by key actors in different sectors and the necessary contexts for creative knowledge work.

Note

1. iPhone (2007) Apple website. [Online]. Available at: http://www.apple.com/uk/iphone// [Last accessed 19th September 2007].

6 Advertising I

Contextualization of the Advertising Sector

This chapter and the next focus on empirical data gathered from the advertising sector. This sector was chosen on the basis of a literature review of creativity where artistic endeavours epitomized this form of activity. Appendix 1 on methodology noted two forms of triangulation: data and theory. These were used to provide coherence and show relational relevance between the theoretical framework and the empirical data using Denzin's (1989) 'levels of person analysis' were framed using the methodological approaches of the two-way relationship between producers/services and users or 'co-configuration' (Victor and Boynton, 1998) and 'epistemic cultures' (Knorr Cetina, 2005a and 2005b). In addition to these, it will also apply a microsociological stance (Knorr Cetina and Bruegger, 2002a) where 'micro and macro' structures are used to provide contrasts and comparisons of creative knowledge application. The data referred to in Chapters 6 and 7 were collected from interviews of practitioners and academics in the advertising sector (Appendix 2 and the related quotations/references are denoted by 'SL', e.g., SL3, at the end). Also included are external sources relating to the sector, and the interdisciplinary theoretical framework provides evidence that is rich and textured. By focusing on the creative application of knowledge at three levels: intra and inter-sectoral, and the influence of creative knowledge working in operational cultures, this and the following chapters will also address the research questions posed at the outset in Chapter 1:

a) What are the characteristics of knowledge work in the sector?
b) What are some examples of this type of knowledge working in the sector under examination?
c) What is the importance of the creative dimension to knowledge work in this sector? And finally,
d) What are the related and requisite skills, abilities, personalities, and contexts necessary for creative knowledge work to occur?

By focusing on the descriptions of style of knowledge work, it is intended to show that common practices of specific roles (e.g., copywriting and creative directing) in advertising across all three countries are not 'nationally bound' but have elements of 'global social forms.' This 'micro' approach to investigating creative knowledge work is used as a guide to build up a case for the existence of the sector. The principle of 'microsociology' offers an interrelational argument where a micro-analysis of creative knowledge application in the sector contains elements of the 'macro' or global context (please refer to Appendix 1 for a fuller explanation of the research methodologies). The micro descriptions in relation to creative knowledge work are examined in this chapter. In the following chapter, related micro dimensions such as the significance of ICET, closer working between producers and users, enculturation processes of this type of work, and macro descriptions of the sector will be discussed.

This chapter has three sections. The first provides an introduction to the advertising sector and the next focuses on the descriptions of creative applications of knowledge in it. The final section offers observations.

Micro Descriptions of Creative Applications of Knowledge in the Advertising Sector

This section discusses the three aspects of the research: a) examples of knowledge working, b) the importance of the creative dimension and c) the related skills, abilities, and personalities of workers.

Creative Application of Knowledge in the Sector

The creative application of knowledge is examined in two types of jobs: copywriting and creative directing. Each of these will be analyzed in terms of the creative work involved, the creative skills, abilities, and personalities required, and the relevant enculturation dimensions such as training, formal and informal education, and ICET. A comparative analysis is offered at the end.

Copywriter

The main function of copywriters is to "write headlines and story line of television commercials" according to a copywriter interviewee (SL 7) who worked for one of the largest advertising agencies in the world (Appendix 3, Table A3.1) based in Japan. Another interviewee (SL4), an academic with advertising experience in England, provided further insights:

> they have to be persuasive in their writing and also be able to articulate. John Hegarty [one of the famous creatives who worked for the BBH agency in London and was responsible for the Levi's 'Refrigerator' commercial] is very good at this. He can sell anything. They [copywriters] have to be able to convince their colleagues their ideas are OK and boss and clients. They have to be persuasive and be able to write but above

all to have ideas. You got to understand the market, the target audience, and that's quite difficult I think and so many people in advertising sell 'purchase side' and then and very often write for women and write about parenting and a variety of women out there doing that.

SL4

Writing a copy for an advertising campaign involved more than just the ability to research and use appropriate words relevant to the campaign. As indicated by interviewee SL4, the manner in which the targeted audience is persuaded is also important. Another academic (SL15), an American with advertising experiences in the US but working at a university in Singapore, said:

A sense of humour and the ability to think visually using visual puns are important for a copywriter so it entails the ability to use words and pictures together to make people smile. I always tell my students that the news is bad such as wars etc. and turning over to the next page [in a print medium such as newspaper or magazine], you have this humorous advertisement and so the ability to visualize it on a more presentable medium is important.

SL15

The ability to write memorable phrases and repeat words in different sentences is an important ability of a copywriter. This can be learnt on the job, in formal education (e.g., in advertising courses) or informally from parents or adults with knowledge of literature and society. The ability to write is one aspect of copywriting and it requires application of knowledge to use words, which people can relate to and which inspires them to want or have a relationship with a product. Some memorable advertising phrases are "Happiness is a cigar called Hamlet"[1] and "Does exactly what it says on the tin."[2]

Below are examples of the emotional connections, which offer intra-sectoral styles of working. Interviewees such as SL2, a creative director at an advertising agency in London, used the term, "to be a general sponge" to denote the acquisition of "knowledge and things that inspire from films and people you hear and things that you see and places that you visit." The President and Creative Director of an advertising agency in Singapore (SL12), (a Singaporean who worked in the US, England, and Asian countries) used the term "social chameleon" to mean:

I think you need to be a social chameleon because a large part of it requires you to sell products to people in small towns (like Grimsby in England), able to think like that person and be able to relate to that person. You need not be pigeon holed. You need to think outside the box. You have to be socially versatile and able to relate to all levels within society. I think that is very important. Secondly, abnormally curious to things in life, to be and wanting to find out why things work. I think you will find this is quite common in all creative people irrespective you are in advertising or a writer. I think these are the two most important ones—social chameleon and curiosity.

SL12

This ability to use emotions/experiences that move and connect the consumer with the product through advertising by creating an emotional bond is important in the application of creative knowledge. Another is the development of an aesthetic 'eye' (Lash and Urry, 1994, p. 123) which is the ability to translate suitable imagery onto a popular medium like the television, for instance, using knowledge of real-life situations and universal story lines. The copywriter from an advertising agency in Singapore (SL13) used the Hamlet cigar campaign[3] to illustrate this. The campaign showed a strong emotional association with a cigar, which was not merely a smoke, but one which provided solace from life's bitter disappointments. In this way, it could be argued that there were emotional dimensions to this campaign, which were heightened by soothing, sad, and timeless music from Bach's Air on a G String. This series of advertisements, started in the 1960s, also had contemporary reference to an affluent professional class. These included a golfer in a sand bunker attempting unsuccessfully to drive his golf ball out of the bunker and the future of manufacturing depicted by an incorrectly assembled robot with its head screwed on the wrong way seeing its image in a mirror, with a Hamlet cigar in its hand. Related to the themes of solace and disappointments and the 'believable' real-life situations, the name of the product was aptly chosen, making a literary reference to Shakespeare's contemplative Hamlet.

How a copywriter displays knowledge and creation of an emotional bond with the audience/users and the product was explained by an academic in England (SL5). He gave the example of the 'Naughty but nice' fresh cream cakes campaign in the 1980s in the UK.[4] The copy itself does not describe or specify the actual product but merely alludes to the self-indulgent enjoyment of the unhealthy product (thus 'naughty'). This implicit comparison between two ideas within the advertisement is portrayed on two levels. The picture depicts two men dressed as drag queens looking at a photo album. The cross-dressing and the reminiscing of their younger and more adventurous days provide the idea of 'naughtiness' and this 'naughtiness' is implicitly equated with the fresh cream cakes. At another level, past 'nice' pleasures of their youth, also hint at the outré decadent preferences of cross-dressing in the 1980s, which are equated with the pleasure of eating cream cakes. These emotional layers created an entertaining television advertisement, which caught the imagination of the audiences. In order to bring together the dimensions in this campaign, the creative workers thus required knowledge of contemporary trends and cultural references as well as being "in tune with the current zeitgeist" as indicated by a practitioner interviewee from an advertising agency in Tokyo (SL8). He described this as follows:

Everything comes down to coming up with a fresh idea. Our job is about building a good relationship between consumers and products/companies.

We need to emotionally touch and connect with people. And to do so, we need a creative idea that is in tune with the current zeitgeist.

SL8

From the above text, it can be seen there are different types of emotional connections and applications of knowledge work by copywriters. These intra-sectoral approaches include: "to be a general sponge," "social chameleon," "emotionally touch and connect" and "in tune with the current zeitgeist." The types of knowledge that are needed include the arts (e.g., literature and films), contemporary events (e.g., golf as a sport in relation to the Hamlet cigar campaign) and life experiences (e.g., "things that you see and places that you visit" (SL12)).

Another type of creative application of knowledge required is the copywriter's ability to anticipate possible popular trends or "anticipatory imagination." This requires not only knowledge of popular and past trends (i.e., being curious and a "general sponge") but also being able to anticipate future trends, and then using this knowledge to create a new form of advertising which taps into and engages with the audience's emotional mood. A practitioner interviewee at advertising agency in London (SL1) explained this approach giving the example of a wood stain and wood-dye product. The carpentry product, Ronseal's 'Does exactly what it says on the tin' campaign, suggested a new trend in ad making. This is because it made a reference to the historical use of the product. The Ronseal copy is clear and to the point about the capability of the product: i.e., the wood stain or wood-dye product will stain or dye the wood effectively. The copywriter used knowledge of current products which was negative, to find a positive spin, and appeal to 'confused' do-it-yourself customers. This campaign not only created a new trend in the sector but the copy also appeared in everyday use.[5] As shown, copywriters need to use their cultural knowledge and act as popular sociologists to hook or entice an audience emotionally to buy a product or positively project a brand image. The copywriter relies on a combination of humour, iconic music, and emotional appeal to ensure that the advertisement is effective.

The above descriptions of creative knowledge application by copywriters offered intra-sectoral insights. Inter-sectoral activities and influences on work cultures will be discussed in the 'Closer working between producers and users in the sector' section in the next chapter. Related to these activities are skills, abilities, and talents, which copywriters require.

In addition to the above, a copywriter also required related attributes. The copywriter who worked for an advertising agency in Singapore (SL13) explained thus:

> You need to have the desire not to get stuck in a regular job. I get bored easily. I wanted to be an artist in school and found it didn't pay that well and I don't want to be a pauper all my life. So I trained for accountancy and personal management and was completely bored with them. I could draw and write and so I went into advertising. Every day is new. The

route to a creative [copywriter] is not usual [via a degree]. My work part-ner here [anonymized] was a bricklayer and a ski instructor before and now in advertising. You need an ego in this business like artists and per-formers: there is an exhibitionist streak in us . . . to succeed you need to sell your ideas, have the ability to get on with other people, good client relationship—for clients to trust you is key. Resilience is important and one needs to separate the personal from the idea . . . We work as a team to bounce off ideas, share responsibility as well as the ability to bounce back.

SL13

The abilities to generate ideas and present them in a persuasive manner through excellent communication skills are important. These communication skills are also required in working with other creatives (such as creative directors and art directors), clients, and other members of the team (such as researchers, account executives, and technical staff). The abilities to cope with rejection and bounce back require a certain level of confidence and perseverance.

Creative director

The main aim of creative directing was explained by a creative director of an advertising agency in London (SL1):

My job is to bring it [advertising campaign] to life, execute it in a way that is potent.

SL1

The campaign may be a television commercial (such as 30 seconds in length), a bill poster in an outdoor location, newspaper, or a pop-up advertisement in a film either in a cinema or on the Internet.

Below are examples of these intra-sectoral workings. The Creative Director (SL1) sets out his vision in the following terms:

The overall idea is centred round the design work and using the design to pump out a lot of promotional messages day in day out. It's much more design rather than copy and word, and the normal advertisement you see in the paper. I don't think people would have dreamt of doing that 10 years ago. That was a new approach to advertising and also launching a brand as well. The work we did for the Automobile Association[6] [AA], where we gave them the strategic thought to think of themselves as an emergency service rather than a breakdown service and also the end line was: 'To our members, it's a fourth emergency service.' That's a strategic idea, which is hard-wired to the creative execution that we adopted over the years. A lot of agencies are now still only interested in the final execution. They almost work backwards and post-rationalise the strategy. Here was a cam-paign where the strategy was decided and became the whole focus of the campaign. We were trying to get at the company's (client's) ethos rather than just a clever advertisement. The idea of the fourth emergency service became part of the company's operation where you can see the person answering the phone.

SL1

Besides offering insights as a creative director, the interviewee also described the creative process of changing strategy during ad making, which is linked to brand making. An example is AA, a television commercial organization, which after following the idea of becoming 'a fourth emergency service,' changed the company's operation from a breakdown service to an emergency one. The vision of the Creative Director was first, to identify the client's (AA) ethos and, second to use it to create an entirely different operation for the organization from one of a breakdown service to one which car users could identify as an essential emergency service similar to that of a fire brigade or ambulance. The creation of this vision of an emergency service included the accessibility via the campaign for car users to visualize frontline staff in uniforms responding to in-coming calls, and reacting quickly by sending out help with flashing lights on the vehicles. These visual images were similar to those created by other emergency services. By relying on other symbols AA could build their own brand. This creative approach not only created a shift in advertising but also changed the operations of AA. Thus, one may suggest that the advertising strategy changed an organization's modus operandi in a different sector, i.e., inter-sectoral approach.

The Creative Director (SL1) used the phrase, "The aura a brand gives off is emotional." This use of emotional connectivity is relevant to creative directing as in copywriting where interviewees from this project—including a creative director of an advertising agency in London (SL2), a creative director in Tokyo (SL8), and the President and Creative Director of an agency in Singapore (SL12) used terms like 'to be a general sponge,' 'in tune with the current zeitgeist,' and 'social chameleon' to describe how workers had to be alert to possibilities and to use this knowledge to keep trying to be different, to push the boundaries and the limits of the medium. Creative workers also had to be curious and questioning and to ask why and be able to capture the "zeitgeist" by reading, listening to music, accessing other forms of the arts and culture, and observing the milieu of everyday life and events.

An example of a commercial that captures the spirit of the time was the 1969 Birds Eye frozen peas campaign featuring the child actress, Patsy Kensit, saying the slogan, "Sweet as the moment when the pod went 'pop'."[7] This advertisement had a jingle accompanying the slogan. One might suggest that Birds Eye's freezing methods managed to maintain the freshness of the product even though the peas were frozen following on from the imagery of the commercial. The customers of this product would be born after World War II, in their twenties, working, and had some disposal income. Their diets in the previous decade, the 1950s, were simple. With the emergence of the post-war baby boom generation, the company might have hoped that potential consumers would be opened to the idea of enjoying a convenient and seemingly fresh product.

Technical knowledge of graphics, typography, and digital-related media is relevant in the role of a creative director. Creative directors, like Joe Pytka, believe that technological advances have meant, "the technical moment has replaced the moment of truth" (Vaske, 2001, p. 258). He suggested that people in the advertising sector should retain the integrity of a storyline and use technology to convey its integrity in "a new and honest way." The development of technology will be expanded later in this section.

Following from Pytka's approach, the descriptions below provide further insights. Creative directors, like the interviewee in London (SL3), provided a description of an intra-sectoral creative process in relation to the application of technology:

> We did a commercial here for Levis which was called "Twist."[8] It is people's arms being twisted round. That was made possible by technology. To some young guys, these are not twisted jeans, they are science jeans with science in front, so let's do an advertisement about twisting. Would it be great if people can twist round their limbs? Twenty years ago, we could not have made that advertisement, as technology for that did not exist. So it's a great example through becoming reality by using technology. It had creative people involved and also those with technical skills. The technical skills are of secondary importance. To have an initial something [idea] and then to make it work in the best way possible and equally the music, a whole army of people creating that, it's like choosing the music: it is a whole subjective judgement. There are people whose job is to find music for commercials. They watch the commercial with no sound and come back with a list of 10 possible music.
>
> SL3

An emotional link with the consumers/users might be through music and, accordingly, knowledge of relevant music genres in relation to the campaign and audience is pertinent.

Technical knowledge is particularly relevant in the age of digital technologies, which affects the advertising sector. In the above example, the technology was applied in a specific manner. In connection with technologies in the knowledge economy, the founder and owner of a local advertising agency in Singapore (SL14) described the specific skills of connecting technologies with advertising as "kinetic interaction." He noted especially that with "young people who are connected to the digital medium and have the ability to learn quickly and have a passion, energy, adventurousness, openness to try new things and are entrepreneurial . . . so training people to be very attuned to the digital medium and managing their own changes" is critical.

In advertising work, technologies and technological artefacts such as mobile phones and laptop computers are used regularly and this use of technology is arguably generic. The significance of ICET in the advertising sector is discussed in the next chapter.

The Levi's "Twist" Jeans campaign described the leadership qualities that were needed for the role of creative directing. A crew is involved in the production of the advertisement from an initial idea to the marketing of the commercial in various media such as posters, newspapers, television, Internet, and films. These include copywriters, art directors, account executives, technicians, and researchers and they may be part of the advertisement agency or sub-contracted. Knowledge of crew members is acquired over a period of time and through experience. The knowledge of the crews' strengths and personalities enables the creative director to bring out the best in each of them towards the objective of producing a successful campaign. Gardner (1999) called these competences as "interpersonal and intrapersonal."

Leadership skills that are needed in the role of a creative director include the ability to a) research and find a relevant idea which is appropriate to the product and the organization's vision, b) convince the client and the crew members that it is a potent concept, and c) strategize and manage the team to deliver the product in a coordinated manner. It is the creative director who "brings it [advertising campaign] to life, and executes it in a way that is potent" (SL1). Additionally, SL1 noted, the creative director needed relevant knowledge and an aesthetic eye. This 'eye' was different from that of a copywriter's, because the director should be able to visualize and imagine the impact of the advertisement and the options possible, either a film or poster. A creative director must to be able to produce visual imagery, either a commercial film, or print, which is truthful and original. This visual reality is not the same as a person's visual reality as most of the commercials are executed on film and thus the imagery is via a camera lens.

Different types of knowledge are required for creative directing. Knowledge of the technical aspects and possible visual impact on different media is crucial. Knowledge of previous advertising experiences is helpful. All of this has implications on the final edited version of a film commercial of 60 seconds. This lens-edited commercial is the creative director's vision of the advertisement's original idea. Knowledge of the general public is crucial so as to be able to connect with them emotionally. A specific insight into the emotional connection in advertising was given by one of the interviewees: the Creative Director of an agency, based in London (SL1), with the Ronseal commercial. The client, a do-it-yourself specialist, wanted a simple and effective message for its customers. In the past, these products were sold on sophisticated branding exercises. The particular creative director and his team came up with this slogan "Does exactly what it says on the tin," which countered the multiplicity, variation, and confusion of previous advertisements. His scene setting comment was:

> it might sound a step backward but it gave its customers a simple message. It is a very powerful and successful ad and has since gone into the language to describe a person, a way of doing things.
>
> SL1

Linking a creative director's creative use of knowledge is anticipatory imagination. It is the ability before filming to visualize the impact the finished commercial product will have on an audience and whether or not they will connect with the commercial emotionally and come away with a sympathetic view of the brand. These brand-creating moments might be humorous, dramatic, or entertaining but they must connect with the audience. Lash and Urry (1994) and Reich (2001) mentioned the use of "semiotics" or signs and symbols, which could add value to a brand. The ability to access knowledge like a "general sponge," rely on previous job experiences such as imagery making, and use relevant knowledge (as described earlier by SL2) to hook an audience through various genre of entertaining are important abilities that a creative director must have. The President and Creative Director of an advertising agency in Singapore (SL12) describes his role as being a "social chameleon" with an emotional connection to the public.

The above descriptions of the intra and inter-sectoral creative applications by creative directors have shown that they have to rely on a wide range of knowledge including that of arts and cultural events (e.g., music for the Levi's Twist Jeans campaign), people's daily lives (e.g., SL12's metaphor of a "social chameleon" and emergency services as in the AA advertisement), social trends or as SL8 noted be "in tune with the current zeitgeist" (e.g., Bird's Eye Frozen Peas and the Ronseal advertisements), technical possibilities (e.g., Levi's Twist Jean campaign), and manage crew members (e.g., camera people, copywriters, account executives, and technical specialists) involved in the campaign. In terms of skills and abilities, these include an aesthetic eye for imagery view through the camera lens (e.g., AA campaign of portraying the organization as an emergency service via frontline staff), and an anticipatory imagination (e.g., Ronseal advertisement and SL1 interviewee's comments). Creative directors also need leadership and management qualities to provide a vision for a campaign (e.g., Ronseal advertisement) and advise clients, because advertising can alter the organization's core activities (e.g., AA). They must also be able to research and choose relevant ideas and strategize in order to facilitate the eventual completion of the advertisement.

Comparison of the Two Creative Jobs on Knowledge Application

This final part compares the characteristics of the two jobs in terms of their creative application of knowledge in the sector, and the skills, talents and personalities in relation to the theoretical framework.

The two roles of the creative knowledge jobs discussed in the previous section have commonalities as well as differences. For a copywriter, it is the use of words/texts for an advertising medium such as television, which will enable connection with the audience. The ability to write and willingness to learn to write are crucial for this job. A creative director has to produce a commercial, usually on film for around sixty seconds, which must be viewed through a camera lens. A creative director also needs to administer, execute, strategize, and motivate the team members to follow directions. Team working is important but more crucially are the leadership talents, to which Sternberg et al. (2004) referred.

An advertisement may be a combination of texts (copy), images (either still or moving), and audio (music). In order to bring into fruition, an advertisement/campaign requires different forms of knowledge from different creative knowledge workers in the sector. Two of these roles, copywriting and creative directing, were micro-analyzed above. The common feature in the two roles is their ability to form emotional connections between the consumer and product. These connections were described by interviewees as "general sponge" (by SL2), "social chameleon" (by SL12), and "in tune with the current zeitgeist" (by SL8).

In order to write a line of text such as "Does exactly what it says on the tin" (Ronseal campaign) and "Happiness is a cigar called Hamlet" (Hamlet cigar campaigns), a copywriter must have knowledge of popular culture, which draws from sources such as literature, films, and current affairs. In the case of the Hamlet cigar commercials (in which there were 58 Hamlet commercials by Collett Dickenson Pearce, London), Rowan Dean and Garry Horner created the 'Photo Booth' Hamlet campaign[9] (Aitchison, 2001). It showed a balding man in a photo booth preparing to have his picture taken by combing his strands of hair rather unsuccessfully. This example of being a 'social chameleon' required knowledge of a famous English sports personality, Sir Bobby Charlton, and the creativity to turn this icon into an entertaining spectacle to which the audience could relate. This campaign, along with the other cigar advertisements, featured the character after a disaster, lighting up a Hamlet cigar with the audio punch line "Happiness is a cigar called Hamlet."

In the case of the Ronseal campaign, the copywriter was familiar with previous campaigns of similar goods, which were complex and required applications of different types of products. The copywriter needed to know the prevailing trend of similar products, "be in tune with the current zeitgeist" (SL8), to come up with a copy which promoted the simplicity of its application as well as its effectiveness.

As indicated above, these forms of knowledge come through the application of emotional connections, popular culture, life experiences, and previous work experiences, and combined they produce what may be called disciplinary knowledge. Some of these are derived from explicit sources such as books and professional advertisement magazines as well as from previous work experiences in ad making, which may be non-codified or tacit.

The above types of knowledge used in advertisement making expand the focus of Knorr Cetina's 'epistemic cultures' (2005a) in areas such as high-energy physics (scientific knowledge) (Knorr Cetina, 2005b) and foreign exchange market (professional knowledge) (Knorr Cetina and Bruegger, 2002b). The epistemic culture of ad making relies on different forms of knowledge as described above: popular culture, life experiences, past work experiences, and both explicit and tacit forms. These forms of knowledge offer a wider variation than those required for high-energy physics and foreign exchange markets. Similarly, the outcomes in the advertising sector are more diverse with different types of campaigns as compared to foreign exchange trading which deals with buying and selling transactions using well-recognized global systems. Lastly, campaigns are driven by the needs of the clients for their products in localized markets unlike the global network, where the foreign exchange markets operate.

Turning to images in a campaign, the role of a creative director is to create a campaign where moving imagery such as a television commercial or a still imagery such as a poster advertisement are produced. An example of a still image was the Silk Cut campaign[10] in the 1990s, which featured a purple silk cloth with a cut. This cigarette campaign, via the emotional connection of being 'a general sponge,' used the knowledge of the paintings of the Italian artist, Lucio Fontana, as a reference point and made a play on the brand. It was also the time when there was a growing public consciousness of the negative health effects of smoking. The only copy on the campaign was the mandatory health warning. In this example, knowledge of the prevailing sentiments of the public and the government as regards to smoking and knowledge of art motivated this campaign.

In the case of a moving image, the AA advertisement offered a new vision and a re-branding where the car rescue organization marketed itself as an additional emergency service as described earlier. The creative director of this television advertisement related his knowledge of emergency services such as ambulance, fire service, and police to the ethos of the organization and the outcome of this campaign resulted in the AA changing its core activity from one of a car rescue operation to an essential service provider.

Music is the third component of a campaign, and it may be relevant in advertisements such as in the Hamlet cigar, which used Bach's Air on a G String. The contemplative music fitted with the disappointment of the individuals portrayed in the campaigns. Knowledge of music is thus also required and research may be carried out by those specializing in music seeking with awareness of different genres. The creative director in particular needs to decide on the appropriateness of chosen music.

From the perspectives of 'epistemic culture' as a methodological approach to investigating the empirical data (Appendix 1), three components are used to create the advertisements. These are: texts, imageries (still or moving), and music. This culture is different to those investigated by Knorr Cetina: high-energy physics (a science-related discipline) and foreign exchange markets (business sector) where they are not present.

Relating to the three components of a campaign with their related forms of knowledge is another type of knowledge that uses technologies. For a creative director, technical knowledge of graphics, typography, and digital-related media are useful and may be called disciplinary knowledge. To some extent, technical-disciplinary knowledge is explicit and can be acquired through formal education such as courses. It may also be tacit and attained through work-based experiences of using and applying knowledge gained in specific contexts. These contexts may require different solutions, which are added to a creative worker's tacit knowledge. The tacit knowledge of past advertising experiences may also be used together with the ability to understand how technologies may be realized in an advertisement. An example of this was the Levi's 'Twist' Jeans campaign where technologies were used to show how young people wearing these jeans were able to carry out impossible movements such as rotating limbs and twisting torsos. The message of these unusual physical movements was not to indicate the wonders of technical applications but to sell the idea that these jeans were manufactured using scientific know-how to fit the wearers' movements: at the core of this campaign was the idea that these were 'science' jeans. The job of the creative director was not to carry out the specific technical activity as this is left to the specialists who needed technical skills to implement the creative design of the campaign. These may be achieved through discussions between the creative director and the technical specialists. In this communication process, the creative director needs to understand and employ the relevant technical terms in order to convey to the specialists the vision of the campaign. There needs to be a level of understanding of the technical terminology and the potential application. In addition to these roles, the creative director needs to anticipate how this technical dimension will be received by the audience or an anticipatory imagination. In short, a creative director needs to be able to capitalize on the technical wizardry.

In relation to Knorr Cetina's (2005a) notion of 'epistemic culture,' technologies offer an important framework for such activities as foreign exchange market trading (i.e., reliance on screens and Internet connections for performing high volume transactions). As described above with advertising, it relates to an understanding of the possibilities of applying technologies to ad making. Technologies are not a main factor but the ability to capitalize on the technical wizardry is. The campaign such as Levi's 'Twist' Jeans uses technologies to highlight the vision of the campaign, which is that the product is a pair of 'science jeans.'

Having different types of knowledge is important but it needs to be applied creatively in areas of: leadership, collaborative working, aesthetic sensibilities, and emotional connections.

Leadership may be related to the role of a creative director, who needs to provide a vision. This vision may be resourced from a variety of means such as knowledge relating to: previous job experiences, knowledge of cultural trends, an attitude of being a general sponge, and the ability to capitalize on technical wizardry. The creative director will need "interpersonal and intrapersonal" abilities (Gardner's idea of multiple intelligences (1999)) to persuade the team of the vision and to motivate them to create an innovative campaign. The creative director of an agency in London (SL1) used his Orange campaign to illustrate this. He suggested that it was "a very multi-disciplined brand launched in multi-national countries in Europe." Emotional knowledge regarding the strengths and weaknesses of the team is also useful in motivating and leading them to a successful campaign. The team members include: copywriters, art directors, researchers, account planners, account executives, and technical specialists. This process requires problem seeking and problem solving abilities in the team.

Collaborative working was an important feature in the two creative roles. This type of work takes place in a distinctive sector with its acknowledged experts and ways of working, which relates to Csikszentmihalyi's (1988) idea of "field and domain." Collaborative working is part of the 'Styles of Working' dimension, which is part of the theoretical framework discussed in Chapter 5. Independent and individual working style was another. Associated with a team working style were skills or 'personal intelligences' (Gardner, 1999), which, according to the creative director at agency based in London (SL3), are not discussed much. His specific insights about this aspect of work are as follows:

> skills are a difficulty—the thing that people do not talk about. Do you know what I mean? Human relational skills and people management are going on all the time but it is not something we can isolate and talk about. This is a difficult one. You just have a feeling with how you deal with their personality. Obviously, we have rows and people get told off for things they have done and shouldn't have done but also they get encouraged when they have done something right or to do something really well . . . it is all those things. In the 40 people, they have different skills as well as personalities and some are more likeable and some less likeable. Some have more experience and some are older or younger. We have strata of people who are straight out of college and those who have been doing this for 12–14 years. So they have to be treated in different ways.
>
> SL3

The roles of creative directors discussed above and in the earlier section on leadership abilities indicate that they must be able to convince the team of their vision for ad creating. The leadership abilities include emotional knowledge of the team in order to elicit the best from each person. Using Orange campaign as an example, the creative director needed to rely on a research team on the variations of audiences across Europe, where the product was targeted. Creating a dialogue was important so that the research team understood the brief and data required in order for the creative director to create a common advertising strategy across Europe.

Related to leadership abilities was collaborative working. As the creative director (SL3) indicated, the ability to engage with, listen, understand, and motivate people in the Orange campaign was relevant to its fruition. Referring to the methodological perspectives of 'co-configuration' (Victor and Boynton, 1998), using the above description as a focus for discussion, it can be argued that the relationship went beyond the producer (client being Orange, a mobile network operator and Internet service provider) and user (consumers of Orange's products and services). The advertising agency acted as a conduit between Orange and its consumers. The client-user relationship was mediated by the agency via its campaign. This three-way relationship may also be expanded to include the team within the agency along with those outside such as sub-contracted groups, which may be involved in researching the audiences in the different European countries. This example offers different forms of relationships from a clearly defined one such as the client-ad agency to a more ephemeral one such as client-sub-contracted groups. It also offers a wider range of stakeholders in a 'co-configuration' relationship. Earlier micro-analysis of ad making through the lenses of copywriter and creative directors also indicate that different forms of knowledge from multi-stakeholders with their specialisms (such as account planner, researchers, and client) are needed to complete an advertisement. The eventual realization of an advertisement as already described above might rely on knowhow using texts, imagery (still or moving), and audio (such as relevant music). These nuanced forms of professional relationships are different to the two-way relationship of Victor and Boynton's.

The creative knowledge workers in this sector such as copywriters and creative directors apply their knowledge through: aesthetic sensibilities and emotional connection with their audiences, as described above. Gardner's (1999) notion of creativity refers to a person asking new questions and doing something novel. A creative director in arriving at a vision from the camera lens perspective needs to use knowledge such as past job experiences, an understanding of the possibilities of technologies, and cultural knowledge (as discussed earlier) to create an effective campaign. This campaign may be unexpected (novel) and come as a surprise to the audience who may be able to relate to it and ask what the audience is not expecting of this advertisement of a product: i.e., ask new questions. Examples of this creative approach might include the AA and the Ronseal advertisements. Another form of creativity, which was exhibited in the production of advertisements discussed above, followed Csikszentmihalyi (1988)'s notion of producing a variation. An example might be in the innovative portrayal in the 'Twist' Levi's jeans advertisement where these garments are marketed as scientifically conceived and manufactured. This is done by showing them worn by people performing outlandish physical movements. This portrayal of unusual physical movements, assisted by technologies, was equated with the 'science' dimension of these jeans (i.e., jeans with a variation).

The innovative approaches to ad making offer an explanation for the diversity of campaigns described in the sections above. This diversity of advertisements offers another difference to Knorr Cetina's (2005b) 'epistemic culture' of foreign exchange trading where global and uniform systems are used to buy and sell foreign exchange currencies.

As regards aesthetic sensibility, discussed in Chapter 2, and in the micro-analysis section, the copywriter must translate it into a suitable medium such as television where the writing will have an impact on the commercial. This sensibility not only needs to move the audience but also needs to be an ear for what resonates with the customers. The creative director's aesthetic eye is in the form of envisioning and producing a visual imagery via camera lens that is true to the original idea. In the two roles, the creative workers need to form an emotional relationship with the audience using the knowledge described above. Metaphors and phrases such as 'to be a general sponge,' 'in tune with the zeitgeist,' 'emotionally touch and connect,' and 'a social chameleon' had been used by the interviewees to describe this emotional relationship. The copywriter applied words to connect with his audience: 'Does exactly what it says on the tin,' and 'You deserve a Break Today.' The creative director at an agency in London (SL1) who was also a former colleague of John Hegarty, provided specific insights about the emotional hook of the Levi's 'Refrigerator' commercial of the man in the launderette, which captured the zeitgeist. He described how John Hegarty layered this commercial with the music by Muddy Waters' 'Mannish Boy' to bring out the character of the film, which Hegarty (Vaske, 2001, p. 156) termed 'film vibration.' The success of the commercial depended upon the emotional connection with the audience and the application of relevant knowledge to create ideas and vision to make a lasting impact. This had to be done by creative directors who worked collaboratively and effectively.

In terms of creative personalities, these differed depending on the role. The copywriter needed to have empathy with the customers of the product, be honest about the product, and build a long-lasting relationship with the consumer from the point of view of brand making. This took confidence and patience through any possible failed attempts to get the best jingle line and some degree of risk taking, which included the "willingness to try and not afraid to fail" as described by the President and Creative Director of an advertising agency in Singapore (SL12). It was noted that the common traits across all the two jobs based on the interviews and relevant literature included "fun, enjoyment and happiness".

A creative director organizes, strategizes, executes, and plans a campaign. This also includes visualizing before filming and persuading team members to do what is required. This requires confidence and unconventionality, the ability to articulate ideas and a vision, as well as emotional sensitivity to cultural trends.

Summary

This empirical chapter on advertising examined two forms of creative applications of knowledge: copywriting and creative directing and identified two approaches: intra and inter-sectoral of creative knowledge work.

Notes

1. Hamlet Cigars—'The Baldy Man'. (2008) [VideoSift]. Available at: http://ww.adslogans. co.uk/hof/hrfindx4.html/. [Last accessed 13th November 2008].

2. Ronseal Advert. (2008) [YouTube]. Available at: http://www.youtube.com/watch?v= PXznmGz2fy4. [Last accessed 13th November 2008].
3. CPD Classic ads—Hamlet Cigars (1966–1997) (2007). [YouTube}. Available at: https://www.youtube.com/watch?v=NickHmwZAeI. [Last accessed 30th November 2012].
4. Fresh Cream Cakes Naughty But Nice advert from the eighties. (no date) [YouTube]. Available at: https://www.youtube.com/watch?v=zswOFJZ4vZE [Last accessed 13th November 2012].
5. Popularity of the expression as evidenced on the Oxford University Press. [Online]. Available at: http://www.oup.com/elt/catalogue/teachersites/oald7/wotm/wotm_archive/tin?cc=gb. [Last accessed 30th November 2012].
6. AA the 4th emergency service (2011) [Vimeo]. Available at: http://vimeo.com/14319519. [Last accessed 2nd May 2014].
7. UK television adverts 1955–1990. (no date). [Online]. Available at: www.headington.org.uk/adverts/food.htm. [Last accessed 30th November 2008].
8. Levi's "Twist": 90 Commercial (2012). [YouTube]. Available at: https://www.youtube.com/watch?v=XbseqMxhoP0. [Last accessed 3rd May 2014].
9. Benson and Hedges—Photo Booth (2008). [YouTube]. Available at: https://www.youtube.com/watch?v=G5zzRYSNvRQ. [Last accessed 3rd May 2014].
10. The history of advertising in quite a few objects: 35 Lucio Fontana's paintings. (26 July 2012) [Online]. Available at: http://www.campaignlive.co.uk/news/1142844/. [Last accessed 3rd May 2014].

7 Advertising II

Introduction

The second empirical chapter on advertising focused on the micro and macro dimensions of creative knowledge work, identified as themes in the theoretical chapters. Following the introduction, this chapter is divided into the following sections: micro dimensions of creative applications of knowledge in the advertising sector, macro descriptions of the sector, and observations and insights.

Micro Dimensions of Creative Applications of Knowledge in the Advertising Sector

This section is divided into four parts namely: significance of ICET, closer working between producers and users, enculturation processes of this type of work, and a summary.

Significance of ICET and the Advertising Sector

The descriptions of the two roles of creative knowledge workers in the previous chapter clearly indicated that ICET has an impact on advertising. Technical knowledge is especially relevant to a creative director and relates to an understanding of (i) how technology affects graphics, (ii) the typology through the use of digital-related media and (iii) not the technical specifications of ICET itself. The emotional connection with the audience is critical and is further enhanced by the creative application of ICET.

The data collected from the interviews showed that both creativity and ICET were critical components in the creative knowledge-making equation. The creative director of an agency in London (SL2) noted:

> It's an interesting question. We talked about this as the Creative Age. I think the knowledge industry is one that has been a technological age and it's happening in business—ways of sharing knowledge and ultimately, to think creatively is a lack of confidence in the technological age. One thing

technology can't do is to think randomly and it can't make us to be entirely logical and we think that humans do have an important part to play.

SL2

Creativity and how relevant knowledge can be applied to design innovative campaigns are paramount factors. The technicians are required to generate the required activities as envisioned by a creative director and this includes appealing to a digital audience. Developments in ICET offer a different advertising engagement with the digital audience, which includes the understanding and application of technical knowledge for the purposes of ad making. The Creative Director (SL3) and colleague of John Hegarty noted the shift in approach and said:

> We talked about it internally quite a lot when it happened and what we were going to do about it. One of the main things that came out of these discussions, was that there was a feeling that technology was in the hands of technicians not in the hands of the creative thinkers and we need to find out about the technology and apply creativity to it without relying on basically people who knew how these things worked. This was quite an important thing. We also decided fundamentally, nothing has changed, it is about having ideas and free thinking and doing unconventional things and thinking out of the box. Those things are all still the same. Our knowledge of brands and consumers are still the same and we need to embrace the technology and become less reliant on technicians.

SL3

Technical specialists or technicians are relied upon in making a campaign. What is different now for the advertising sector is the ability for workers such as a creative director to understand how technologies may be applied to a campaign to execute a vision. In short, the workers in this sector need technical wizardry, which enable a product in the marketplace to become distinguished through advertising. As in the Levi's 'Twist' Jeans campaign, it was to portray the product as 'science jeans' where the wearer could make contortionist poses without splitting the jeans. It was the elasticity of the material which marked the product as 'science jeans.' Technology was used to create an image for the product, and it was the job of the creative director to envision and implement this in relation to the campaign.

The founder of an advertising agency in Singapore (SL 14) called for "training people to be very attuned to digital medium." This reaction to advertising due to technological advancement does alter the nature of the commercial as in the 'Twist' Levi's[1] advertisement. This added dimension impacts on how advertising creative workers think about the end product of a commercial. They use their anticipatory imagination to imagine how new technologies can influence the advertising idea and the reaction of the audience. The notion of being a general sponge also plays a part in this. Finally, they use their imaginations to ascertain the various media outlets for this campaign.

Besides these technical aspects, there are five other features that contribute to the way in which different audiences engage with advertising. These are: increasing technology-based media platforms such as mobile phones, tablets (e.g., iPad), and Internet television (e.g., 4oD and iPlayer); differing screen sizes; multi-tasking facilities; temporal dimension; and heightened exposure to advertising, e.g., product location and pop-ups.

The proliferation of technology-based media platforms offers greater choices of when, how, and which forms of visual and audio entertainments can be accessed. The audience is no longer captive and predisposed to devote their attention to advertisements. The visual impact of advertisements may vary depending on viewing screen sizes from cinema to a mobile phone. The manner in which advertisements may be viewed is different in the age of the Internet where a person can multi-task with several windows on a screen offering differing forms of entertainment (e.g., on demand programmes and YouTube) or networking (e.g., Facebook) simultaneously. The duration of advertisements may also vary from a usual 60-seconds campaign on a television screen in between a programme or film sections to a shorter timescale for a pop-up on a webpage. Finally, a targeted consumer is exposed to increasing forms of advertising such as product located in a programme, advertisement during breaks and in gaming, and pop-up advertisement on Internet sites.

These developments challenge creative knowledge workers to capture the attention of multi-tasking audiences. In this digital age, creative knowledge working is even more important because it is about engaging with targeted audiences. This shortening of the space in a temporal dimension has implications for creative knowledge approaches in the forms of visual, audio, and emotional connections.

From the methodological approach of 'epistemic cultures,' the proliferation of digital platforms highlights how technologies play a part in ad making and add another layer of complexity to the practices of advertising sector, in addition to some of the others such as emotional connection and aesthetic sensibilities described earlier.

In order that these creative activities are carried out, the acquisition of relevant knowledge, which is to 'capitalize on the technical wizardry' in ad making is crucial as it relates to technical areas, past job experiences, or cultural trends. Creative workers need all the knowledge at their disposal in order to seek and solve the problem of an idea. Emotional connections must be made within seconds with the targeted audience so as to catch their limited attention span. Using the notion of an aesthetic eye, a copywriter needs to create an iconic short copy (this is the use of "semiotics" as described by Lash and Urry, 1994, p. 137 and Reich, 2001, p. 48 in Chapter 2). This is particularly challenging for a copywriter in the age of fast communications. A shorter copy would be preferable, which could instantly connect emotionally with an audience. A trend may be towards imagery (including signs and symbols) rather than text. In this case, a creative director would need to come up with a lens-edited image. For a shorter advertisement, perhaps a sign/symbol such as the Silk Cut campaign with a single cut on a purple silk cloth in the 1980s[2] could convey tacit copy and visual imagery.

In summary, the age of digital technologies offers new resources (such as advanced software and related skills and abilities) and challenges (such as the five digital-related features described above) for creative workers to take into account in their ad-making activities. The collective effect is to heighten the significance of how workers carry out the creative application of their knowledge. The job of a technician is not to create a vision for a commercial but to assist creative workers such as a creative director to realize his/her vision for an advertisement in the eventual visual format. In order to do this, a creative director needs to have an understanding and the ability to visualize the potential applications of the technologies to completing an ad campaign. This knowledge of and ability to capitalize on the 'technical wizardry' also includes an understanding of the potential applications of the proliferation of digital platforms in the contexts of differing screen sizes, multi-functionality of artefacts such as mobile phones, temporal dimension, and heightened exposure to advertising. These are the added complexities that technologies bring to bear on the creative working in the sector.

Closer Working between Producers and Users in the Sector

This section investigates the various perspectives of the relationships between creative knowledge workers in the advertising sector with their clients, users, and relevant stakeholders.

There appear to be three trends. One relates to the use of focus groups within the sector itself (intra-sectoral), the second refers to the creative applications, which may change the culture or the ways in which other agencies in the sector operate, and the third refers to impact creative applications in this sector may have on other sectors/areas of business activities (inter-sectoral).

The applications of knowledge discussed in the previous chapter offer insights into the creative activities in this sector, especially those of copywriting and creative directing. These activities in the main are viewed as intra-sectoral. However, one area not yet discussed in this type of creative knowledge work relates to the use of focus groups. Focus groups of usually ten or less are used by advertising agencies to gauge views and voices of a targeted audience. This approach is used as part of a research and information gathering process as described by interviewees such as SL1 and SL3. There are also agencies which rely on inspirational ideas and not research-driven knowledge to come up with an idea or concept for a campaign. This approach of gathering information enables the designer to make sure that potential users of the product/service can closely relate to the advert. In this case, the gathering of focus group data is carried out by advertising agencies and not necessarily the brand or product companies. This information gathering activity offers a different perspective of the producer-user relationship as described by Victor and Boynton (1998) and appears to be one where information is elicited from focused groups for production of a campaign. The information elicited would hopefully provide representative views of the targeted audience of a specific campaign and would then be factored into the ad-making equation along with data and ideas from other specialist sources such as copywriters, account executives, technical specialists, clients, and other crew members. Examples of such collaborative working such as the Levi's 'Twist' Jeans, Ronseal, and the AA campaigns have been described in the earlier chapter. The relationships between creative workers and their clients are described below.

The second type of application of knowledge in this creative sector relates to the influence of creative working on the cultures in which workers operate. From the sixteen interviews in the advertising sector, professionals and related academics mentioned the way their activities influenced how other campaigns were carried out through the use of various phrases to describe the processes such as "golden thread" (SL4), "potency" (SL2), "total communications approach" (SL16), "three dimensional trust" (SL1), and "green credentials" (SL1 and SL13). These approaches of relating and linking creative knowledge work with the products/services which are being advertised or branded depends on the clients which are organizations with diverse values and visions. This relationship may be described as follows:

> The marketing and creative strategies—what my colleagues call the golden thread—if you have the golden thread that goes through everything leading to your big idea . . . Yes, what you're saying before about interactivity and the now the buzzword is integrated. All of that advertising has to be integrated, media is integrated and the message is integrated. Doing an advertising campaign years ago you might use one advertising agency for advertisement for TV, radio or magazine and another agency in Watford in the back streets, would do everything else. But now, agencies do everything themselves or they integrate with sister companies or different departments or whatever to make sure that whatever idea they have goes right across all the media that's used whether you're getting a leaflet through your letter box, or an advertisement in the bus or on your petrol muzzle or TV or cinema, it's coming to you with the same message. A good example is Orange campaign. Everybody knows Orange and they've got Orange leaflets through your door, Orange posters and Orange press advertisements—a whole message. That's an integrated campaign. That's what they want now and I think they also want people—integrated people. People who can, do it. A lot of agencies are going away from separate departments and much more to having teams. So if you are in a team, if you have the understanding of everybody else in your team what they're doing in sight, makes you better teamwork."
>
> SL4

The academic in England was using the concept of the 'golden thread' to describe a particular approach used by more and more agencies. This integrated approach to ad making was illustrated by the Orange campaign as espoused by the creative director of a London advertising agency (SL1). Another creative director from London (SL2) used "potency" to explain her agency's relationship with its clients (e.g., John Lewis Partnership):

> The focus group has become the buzz word even for the government [New Labour]. We don't use it for creativity but to acquire knowledge. Thus xxx wanted it to be more potent and try and use creativity and to get further into the hearts of our clients and help them to crack problems. Often clients come to us having decided to do advertising and to communicate to their customers may use it to rectify something or to advertise a new product. Once you get this, there is very little you can do apart from something they would like or acquiesce. It's much more potent to be involved with the people in the business before they get to the stage where they want to do advertising. We are not a creative ad agency but we are a marketing agency. Marketing is an accepted part of my business now where the advertising is one bit of what they do. We ended up having lots of close relationships with managing directors and chairman and that what we find that we can share information and have a bigger picture.
>
> SL2

The above agency offers a bigger business approach, which includes more than just advertising a product or a service for its clients. Again, the Creative Director offers insights of this approach in relationship to some of its clients:

> The most important thing is big ideas and we can use them in whatever way our clients want like British Telecom [BT] include the ideas in their speeches to the City or in the case of Clarks [a privately owned shoe company], use the ideas in their staff training etc. So it informs how they communicate to each other and to consumers. It's creating a brand by our clients: living and breathing it—the idea. In the case of BT, lots of consumer ideas and internal communication ideas begin with and then spin out. From the big idea, it can manifest itself in innovations.
>
> SL2

This two-way relationship is used to underpin the creative knowledge working between the agency and its clients, staff, and customers. The 'potent' relationship offers a nuanced perspective to that of Victor and Boynton's (1998), which is one between producer and user. This relationship relates to a longer perspective of client-agency engagement before the advertising stage and to a branding activity where the agency identifies an idea or vision, which the client may use before and beyond the advertisements. This approach creates a closer working relationship and this creative application includes creating a vision for a campaign (e.g., BT and Clarks) to emotionally connect with its audience (such as 'in tune with the current zeitgeist') and applying relevant technologies and music (in campaigns such as Levi's 'Twist' Jeans and John Lewis Partnership campaigns).

Another culture-changing perspective is one where advertising and marketing activities are merged with a wider range of marketing platforms. In an interview, an academic from a university in Singapore (SL16) used the term, "total communications approach" to explain this creative application of knowledge:

> Agencies or marketing related organizations are moving towards the concept of a total communications approach and not make the lines too distinct between the advertising and public relations agencies. So those joining them must be multi-faceted in the discipline area. So we need to be able to report in print, web, television etc. In the advertising sector, we are moving towards online advertising, web-based promotion, relationship management, whether it is interpersonally or online, direct marketing . . .
>
> SL16

Using a nuanced perspective of a two-way relationship as a methodological approach to exemplify creative knowledge work, the "three dimensional trust" (3DT) approach by the Creative Director of an agency in London (SL1) offers a further example of change in culture/practice in the advertising sector:

> In terms of knowledge being much more readily to everyone, it can make brands more vulnerable. One area we are very keen on is to try and engender a three dimensional trust for a brand whereby the company markets their brands knows they have got to be aware that they can't source cheap products from the developing countries. People will know that due to free flow of knowledge and the possible association with damage to the environment etc. In the old days, first brands came about with one-dimensional trust, which was: I am marketing this to you and it should taste good and that's the trust. You buy into it. Now it is much more than that.
>
> SL1

The establishment of this cultural practice involving clients (and their contracted-out producers), advertising agencies, and potential users as suggested by the Creative Director (SL1), led onto a discussion on ethics in response to whether or not 3DT made advertising more difficult:

> Either more difficult or easier. If you're working with green field sign company like Egg [ethically conscious banking organization] they can put out their stall as part of their mission. For the old economy clients, they may not have such a squeaky clean record. From our point of view, we will try and get these companies to get up the green ladder as far as

possible. But there are people we don't work with for example tobacco companies. Our intent is trying to get them up rather than down.

SL1

The green approach to advertising was also expressed by the Copywriter of a Singapore agency (SL13) when he said:

> I believe in simple living and in consumerism and would like to use this industry to promote good values in order to change people's perceptions. One of our great heroes was Tibor Kalman who did the United Colors of Benetton campaigns.[3] One can argue it is controversial and shocking but it did raise the public awareness in certain issues by using a corporate medium. Thus using corporation money for a good cause. In the future, what I like to see is to credit people from fashion, architecture, design and art in the advertising industry sell good values for example do we need more shopping malls, another computer, another brand of milk? If we look at the amount of resources and money it has gone into the real cost of these products and not just manufacturing costs but also the opportunity cost for example the cost of the rainforest which are destroyed and we have a responsibility towards the earth.

SL13

An example of this are the campaigns of United Colours of Benetton, an Italian clothing company, which in the 1990s were controversial because of their ethical stance on issues of the day such as HIV, capital punishment, and religious reconciliation.[4] Inclusion of an ethical dimension offered the possibility of a nuanced multiple forum engagement between producers or clients of advertising agencies and agencies and/or users or consumers of the products. This indirect interaction can be called 'suggestive branding' because it signals to potential users and the public the ethical or moral stance taken by the producers of the products and this allows a deeper connection with the public. This relates to the interviewee's (SL8) use of the metaphor, 'in tune with the current zeitgeist' in the earlier section.

The third type of creative knowledge work refers to the inter–sectoral variety. The example includes:

> The advertising market in Japan is shaky now [following the economic recession of the 1990s] and there are no new commodities [products] like the Walkman and thus advertisements are not sought after as previous decade. As a result, there are no new clients but the existing clients such as the mobile phone and car tyre companies are still making spending money on commercials and producing them together in order to create a new or more diverse market. Examples of such collaborative ventures include Suntory [drinks company] and AU [mobile company], and Kao

[commodities company such as shampoo] and Toyota [car manufacturer]. The main purpose of such collaborations is to create product brands rather than waiting for companies to come to us. It is a new type of marketing to find new customers, which the companies of the products and services couldn't have done under their own brands. This was because of the depressed market due to the long economic recession. It is an experiment as it is also the first for our clients and us.

SL7

The copywriter of an advertising agency in Tokyo (SL7) offered examples of collaborative campaign-making, which involved the advertising of the clients' products in a combined campaign. The aim was to create a new market at the time of difficult economic conditions of the 1990s in Japan. This inter-sectoral activity of creative ad making was reinforced by the President and Creative Director of an agency in Singapore (SL12) where he described the famous Japanese singer from the boy band, SMAP (an acronym for Sports Music Assemble People[5]), which was featured in advertisements for various products relating to deodorant, whiskey, etc. Lastly, an academic from a university in Singapore (SL15) recounted another inter-sectoral feature of creative knowledge work, which related to the advertisement campaign for recruits of the Republic of Singapore Navy. It used an interactive video game, which could be downloaded from the Internet and sent on to the navy. The use of games, which forms another sector of investigation in the next empirical chapter, offers insights into how advertising is used in other sectors.

The above descriptions offer examples of creative knowledge applications in relation to intra-sectoral (e.g., focus group activities), inter-sectoral (e.g., campaign relating to multi-clients' products) and changes in cultural practices (e.g., 'total communications approach' and 'three-dimensional trust'). From the perspective of Victor and Boynton's (1998) co-configuration methodological approach, the descriptions offer nuanced and modified perspectives. The focus group activities relate to information gathering of consumer views by advertisement agencies on behalf of their clients. The aim is to find an idea/vision for a campaign. An agency may also rely on other sources such as popular culture and current social trends (as exemplified by the metaphor 'in tune with the zeitgeist'), which may come from crew members such as copywriter, art director, and planner of the campaign. The idea and the visual realization of an advertisement, i.e., the processes of concept formation, are reliant on the specialist roles and related forms of knowledge of the creative workers. The changes of cultural practices examples offer a different perspective of the 'co-configuration' two-way relationship. The 'three-dimensional trust' approach involved a wider range of stakeholders other than producer (i.e., client in relation to the advertising industry) and user (i.e., consumer of a product). It involved the manufacturer of the product, employed by the client, advertising agency as a go-between, the user, and the wider public. The brand-making relationship may not be direct but it is based on emotional connection.

The creative director of an agency in London (SL1) described this relationship, as "The aura a brand gives off is emotional." Lastly, the 'multi-clients' products campaign offers a multi-dimensional relationship between clients, advertising agency, and users. This relationship, like the previous example, is not necessarily direct but is based on an emotional connection.

Enculturation Process and Creative Application of Knowledge in the Sector

This section discusses training, work environment, and education, both formal and informal aspects; these are linked to the theoretical framework presented in Chapter 5. The framework drew on Csikszentmihalyi (1988), Zuboff (1988), Drucker (1993), Nonaka and Takeuchi (1995), and Reich (2001). External factors influencing the working context are explored and the ways in which enculturation contributes to the creative application of knowledge are discussed. This section identifies how knowledge may be acquired and skills such as writing for copy may be fine-tuned.

Training for the two creative types discussed earlier takes various forms. A copywriter needs skills in the art of writing, which facilitates and sparks an emotional connection with the audience. The copywriter of an agency in Tokyo (SL7) described this training process, as drafting and re-drafting a sentence. He offered specific insights of the agency's in-house training sessions:

> They [copywriters] are trained in-house where in one session, they have to make one hundred headlines for one year. It's good for creatives. One hundred headlines are one hundred viewpoints. The sources of such viewpoints included research, inspiration, and family-based experiences.
>
> SL7

Based on this interview, it appears that on-the-job training is sufficient, and as such a formal qualification is not a prerequisite for copywriting or creative directing. Without specifically referring to the sixteen interviews conducted, it seems that having a degree is not viewed as important whereas the opposite was true for those wanting other advertising jobs such as account planning. The Course Leader of the Postgraduate Diploma in Advertising (SL4) in a college in England who had worked in the industry said this:

> If somebody comes in as a creative, a degree is still not essential still looking at people's creativity. You have to have a book of work—a portfolio—and in there you put examples of your work, a cross-section of your work, it doesn't have to be work that has been published it's your ideas to show you have ideas and that is how they will judge you.
>
> . . . And this quality could equally come from somebody who haven't got any academic background. I used to teach on the copywriting course and one of the best students I ever had—he worked in a fairground—somebody

who jumps on the dodgems and takes the money. He always wanted to write. He turned out to be very good. Some of the top creative people of today probably work their way up from absolute nothing.

SL4

Some of the interviewees acknowledged that this on-the-spot training offered a way of acquiring the creative skills and techniques though the rate of take-up of these skills might vary from individual to individual. The 'trainees' creative skills might be fine-tuned as they gained in experiences working on various campaign projects. This informal training approach also had its downsides. The same academic quoted above indicated that getting constructive feedback in the industry was difficult and having a supportive mentor was not common. As there are no rules to creative advertising, having the tenacity and confidence to bounce back were considered important characteristics for a creative knowledge worker.

In relation to wider engagement with the sector, SL4, also set up advisory panels as a means to further involve relevant stakeholders, which included advisors from industry (e.g., creative directors from advertising agencies) and related organizations (e.g., Institute of Practitioners in Advertising) to track and reflect requirements of work trends in her accredited programmes. This further involvement of relevant stakeholders offers another perspective of the co-configuration methodological approach, where a wider network of people and organizations (other than producers and users) form a learning and teaching hub for aspiring workers.

As regards some of the necessary skills, the interviewees suggested: presentation, communication skills, team working, and technical skills relating to production and design. Some of the academics interviewed advocated sessions on fine-tuning skills, which may be used in collaborative working to improve communication and team working skills. Opportunities to present ideas or projects could improve presentation skills and occasions to research from a given advertising brief and the use of case studies could improve analytical, problem solving, and strategy-making skills. These advertising-related courses might also cover the wide range of activities required in the industry such as visual and digital-related media and account planning. Industry placements could also provide real experience of the business.

Much has been written about in the previous chapter regarding the need to emotionally connect with the audience in creative advertising. Interviewees such as SL2, SL12, and SL8 discussed informal education/training, which was to acquire knowledge, either tacitly or explicitly, for future use. Informal education resources included: reading books and magazines on popular culture, history, philosophy, art, psychology, sports, music, drama, watching films and television, looking at other forms of visual art, travelling, and being involved in activities that enabled a better understanding of human nature. Supportive parents can assist this informal education as suggested by Reich (2001, p. 49).

Enculturation influences the manner in which teams and individuals apply their knowledge to innovate. The implications for learning and training will be discussed in Chapter 10.

Summary

Using the methodological approaches of: co-configuration and epistemic culture, and the empirical data, this section: a) investigated the rich and textured examples of three types of creative application of knowledge: intra-sectoral, inter-sectoral, and change of cultural/practices, b) discussed the significance of ICET, c) provided evidence for a closer working between producers and users, and d) examined the enculturation required in creative knowledge application.

The micro-analysis of creative knowledge working in advertising suggested that there may be a degree of commonality in the execution of campaigns irrespective of where workers are based nationally or internationally. This commonality relates the use of emotional connections as described by interviewees as "a general sponge" (SL2), "to be in tune with the current zeitgeist" (SL8), and "social chameleon" (SL12). Using emotional connections does not mean, however, that advertisements such as McDonalds are universal. In terms of inter-sectoral ways of ad creation, these included: the AA campaign as recounted by SL1, multi-clients' products campaign as described by SL7, and the use of video gaming for the recruitment of Navy personnel as recounted by the academic, SL15. There were also examples from the changes in cultural practices such as the use of 'potency' as advocated by SL2, the closer working relationship with clients in the execution of an advertisement as discussed by SL10, and the ethical approach as described by SL13. Related to all of these was the impact of technologies and how they created additional complexities towards the final execution of advertisements. These micro descriptions may be operated in England, Japan, or Singapore.

In terms of the methodological approach of 'co-configuration,' the two-way relationships as identified here were nuanced and modified versions of Victor and Boynton (1998). Advertisement agencies may be viewed as an intermediary to clients and consumers. Within this triangular relationship are degrees of professional workings ranging from a clear to a more ephemeral variety. Also, a wider range of stakeholders is identified.

After discussing the methodological approach of 'epistemic culture' in the advertising sector, this section discussed some commonalities and differences with Knorr Cetina's (2005b) 'epistemic culture' in relation to foreign exchange markets. One commonality was the circulation of knowledge within the advertising community, which concurred with Grabher's (2004) study of the advertising community in London, where clients played a central role in the nature of the advertisements, which was governed by the localized requirements of the clients and by the nature of the products in determining the outcomes of the campaigns. His typology of network practices: communality (lasting and intense relationships between clients and agencies);

connectivity (transient and weak networks between clients and agencies); and sociality (ephemeral and intense working relationships between clients and agencies) offered a discussion and access into creative knowledge application in the sector. However, as indicated by the examples of the changes to cultures/ practices in the section, 'Closer working between producers and users in the sector,' creative knowledge work can be placed on a continuum from 'communality' at one end to 'connectivity' at the other.

As regards differences to Knorr Cetina's (2005b) 'epistemic culture' (such as foreign exchange markets), the advertising sector shows the following trends: a wider range of knowledge in ad making, greater diversity of outcomes/ campaigns, localized requirements of clients, styles of advertisements suited to the specific nature of product, less reliance on technologies as a means to achieving the vision for a campaign, and continuing reliance on emotional connections, imagery, and music.

Macro Perspective of the Advertising Sector

This section is based on the microsociology methodological approach by Knorr Cetina and Bruegger (2002a, p. 909) mentioned at the start of the previous chapter. The micro-analysis from the previous section and the preceding chapter offered different approaches to creative working in the advertising sector. These have implications beyond the immediate context towards a global dimension. This section discusses the global dimension or the Macro.

The Macro section includes analysis of the significance of a sector in terms of its size, presence of global advertising agencies, and global brands.

Global Size of the Advertising Sector

The world advertising expenditures[6] for 2000 and 2011 were US$338.9 billion (B) and US$483.B respectively. These figures showed a 43 per cent growth. In regional terms, North America remained the largest advertising spending region (US$131.2B in 2000 and US$165.1B in 2011) followed by Europe (US$92.2B in 2000 and US$134.8B in 2011) and the Asia/Pacific (US$74.0B in 2000 and US$132.2B in 2011). In terms of percentage increase of advertising expenditure by region for the period 2000 to 2011, North America grew by 26 per cent, Europe by 46 per cent, and Asia/Pacific by 79 per cent.[7]

The share of global advertising expenditure by medium as a percentage in 2011[8] was as follows: television (40.2%), newspapers (20.2%), Internet (16.0%), magazines (9.4%), radio (7.1%), outdoor (6.6%), and cinema (0.5%). The forecast for 2013[9] indicated a general percentage increase for all seven media except for magazines with a decrease of 4.1 per cent.

ZenithOptimedia[10] explained the Internet as being the fastest predicted growing medium from 2010 to 2014 resulting from the use of social media and online video advertising. The rise in advertising expenditure on the Internet is at the expense of the fall in advertising expenditures of newspapers and magazines media. In terms of outdoor advertising, its projected increase share was explained by the installation of digital billboards including eye-catching advertisements, short turnover of advertisements, and interaction with consumers (e.g., text messages to consumers' mobile phones, or using motion sensors to react to their movements).[11] These trends toward technologies and a growing proliferation of digital platforms supported the empirical evidence explored in the earlier section.

Global Significance of Advertising Agencies

The last few decades have witnessed the rise of this industry by advertising organizations becoming listed companies and by mergers and acquisitions of others. These financial activities have accounted in part for the global nature of this sector. Using revenue as a more accurate measure than billings (Cappo, 2003), the top five advertising organizations for the two years, 2001 and 2008, in terms of revenue were dominated by the same agencies with slight movements in the top three positions (Appendix 3, Table 3.1). These (in 2008, with comparable rankings in 2001) in revenue size were: 1) WPP Group, 2) Interpublic Group, 3) Omnicom Group, 4) Publicis Group, and 5) Dentsu with their headquarters in the following countries: UK, US, US, France, and Japan, respectively.

In terms of revenue (US$M) growth for the two years, 2001 and 2008, on the whole there were increases in the top two slots: 8,165 in 2001 to 12,694 in 2008 for the largest agency; and 7,981 in 2001 to 12,383 in 2008 for the second largest agency. This was a 55% increase for both. Some agencies experienced decrease in revenues (US$M.) in this period such as those which occupied the following rankings: 3 (7,404 in 2001 and 6,554 in 2008), 6 (2,733 in 2001 and 2,200 in 2008), and 9 (874 in 2001 and 547 in 2008).

Looking at the end of the period 2001 to 2008, the pattern for the top 25 largest agencies other than the largest five, had changed in three ways. The first was the appearance of three new agencies, which specialized in digital-related advertising such as Microsoft Corporation (formerly Avenue A/Razorfish) at position 14, IBM Interactive at 17, and Sapient Interactive at 19. The trend towards digitalization illustrated the growing importance and influence of Internet technologies in the advertising sector. As discussed in the theoretical chapters, (Chapters 2 to 5) the accelerated reliance on ICET in knowledge working was a critical stimulus.

The second was the appearance of 14 agencies in 2008, which were not featured in the top 25 List in 2001. This might be due partly to the takeover of some top 25 agencies such as Grey Global Group (ranked number 7 in 2001) and Cordiant Communications Group (8) by WPP; Digitas (14) by Publicis Group; and Daiko Advertising (16) and Yomiko Advertising (22) by Hakuhodo DY Holdings. The disappearance of these agencies enabled the inclusion of new agencies.

The third way was the inclusion of agencies mainly from the G7 countries such as US (represented by 8 agencies in the top 25 list), Japan (3), UK (3),

France (2), Germany (1) and Canada (2). In addition, there were multiple agencies from countries such South Korea, Brazil, Australia, and Sweden at the end of the 2001 and 2008 period.

These advertising organizations operated globally with the largest agencies having offices in a variety of geographical and cultural settings.[12] They include: BBH (with eight offices worldwide), McCann Erikson (part of Interpublic), Dentsu, Hakuhodo and Saatchi and Saatchi (part of the Publicis Group).

Global Presence of Brands

Another indicator of the global presence relating to this industry is the client for which advertising agencies act. The Top 100 World's Most Valuable Brands in 2003 and 2012 (Appendix 3, Table 3.2) provide a sense of the ever-growing presence of global operations. The top ten brands have a staggering value[13] of US$386.7B. in 2003 and US$ 543.8B in 2012. The 41 per cent increase over the nine-year period reflected the global recession, which came to a head in September 2008. The total value of the largest ten brands from the 2012 List represented 39 per cent of the total valuation of the top 100 global brands. The total valuation for 2012 amounted to US$1,384.6B. To provide some indication of the magnitude of the valuation of the top 100 global brands in relation to a country's GNI (in 2011, the nearest equivalent year), Spain, ranked twelfth largest economy in the world, had a GNI of US$1,428.3B.[14] Even ignoring the discrepancy of comparative years and currency conversion differences, in terms of the largest 100 global brands, this is a significant sector.

These brands operate in an international market and require advertising agencies with a global reach. The worldwide spread of these agencies does not necessarily offer a unified global advertising campaign, but it offers the capabilities to operate in different countries and market conditions. The micro-analysis in the earlier sections offered rich descriptions of ad making in such 'localized' markets as England (e.g., AA campaign), Japan (e.g., Suntory (drinks company) and AU (mobile company)) and Singapore (e.g., SingaPorridge in McDonald's campaign). This tension between global and local offers a varying methodological perspective of Knorr Cetina's (2005a) 'epistemic culture' where professional knowhow of the foreign exchange markets is highly globalized and technologically-based. This is in contrast to agencies, where perhaps globalized financial systems are in place for each agency, but local offices carry out ad making in accordance to local clients' products and needs. These localized approaches to creating campaigns have been described in the previous chapter. This approach might mean agencies having offices in geographical locations which might be majority owned, joint ventures, or minority owned and competing with local independent agencies.

Four trends might be discerned from the top 100 world's most valuable brands. The first trend related to the growing significance of digital brands in the two years of comparison. Google, Amazon, eBay and Facebook appeared in the 2012 period at number 4, 20, 36, and 69, respectively. Of these four digital brands, only Amazon had a presence in 2003 as ranked number 74. The second was the dominance of IT-related brands in the top twenty positions in 2012. They included: Apple (at number 2), IBM (3), Microsoft (5), Intel (8), Cisco (14), Hewlett-Packard (15), and Oracle (18). The third was the relative instability of the top 25 brands over this period with seven changes in the rankings. There were Apple (from number 50 in 2003 to 2 in 2012), Google (from unranked to 4), Louis Vuitton (from 45 to 17), Amazon (from 74 to 20), H&M (from unranked to 23), and SAP (from 35 to 25).

The final trend referred to the 32 new entries in the 2012 List, which did not feature in 2003. Six of the new brands were in fashion and luxury goods (such as H&M, Zara, Gucci, Cartier, Burberry, and Ralph Lauren), five were in motor vehicles (Hyundai, Audi, Porsche, Kia, and Ferrari), and five were in drinks (Sprite, Jack Daniel's, Johnny Walker, Corona Extra, and Heineken). In addition, there were five new brands related to the financial services (Allianz, Visa, Santander, Mastercard, and Credit Suisse), four were in digital-related businesses (Google, eBay, Facebook, and Adobe), three was in engineering and building sectors (Siemens, 3M, and John Deere), and one each in communications (Blackberry), transportation (UPS), and baby products (Pampers).

Summary

This Macro section provided evidence of an established existence in terms of the size of the sector, the global presence of advertising agencies, and the international presence of brands. Alongside the universality, ICET is a significant feature in the trends towards digital advertising, digital-related agencies, and ICET-related brands. However, the presence of advertising activities in terms of its size, the extensive network of international offices and agencies, and the global influence of major brands, does not necessarily mean that ad making is entirely homogenous. McDonald's 'SingaPorridge' campaign is an example. There are commonalities in the use of emotional connections in creative knowledge working as discussed in the previous chapter. However, the emotional connections (such as "a general sponge" (SL2), "to be in tune with the current zeitgeist" (SL8), and "social chameleon" (SL12) are used differently at the local level. An example was given by the Creative Director in Singapore (SL12), who had worked in the US, England, and in several Asian countries. He illustrated this by the Volkswagen Car advertisement in the UK, which was based on Keats' poem, 'Ode to a Grecian Urn' to eulogize about the product. He (SL12) remarked, "but [this] will not work in Asia as it loses the subtleties and nuances in translation." He used the "social chameleon" metaphor to describe the creative director's understanding of the knowhow of people (in this example, the literary knowledge of one of the Romantic poets in England) and the application of this knowledge to use a literary reference to relate it to a car. This literary reference if applied to an audience in Singapore, according to the interviewee (SL12), would not be effective. He used his anticipatory imagination and local knowledge of the public in Singapore to realize the inapplicability of this approach. This illustrated the localized advertisement making approach in this sector as opposed to the globalized approach of the foreign exchange markets (Knorr Cetina, 2005b).

From the perspective of inter-sectoral approaches of ad making, local contexts appeared to dictate the style of campaigns. For example, the multi-clients' products ad making in Japan as recounted by the Copywriter (SL7) and the Art Director (SL9) was not found in either England or Singapore, perhaps due possibly to different ethical approaches in those two countries. However, in terms of the changes in cultural practices, there appeared to a degree of global awareness as regards environmental issues. This awareness was espoused by the Creative Director (SL1) and the Copywriter (SL13). However, this creative application was made in response to the needs of local audiences and clients.

Observations and Insights

This chapter on advertising in the Micro dimensions and the Macro section identified three approaches to creative knowledge work: intra and inter-sectoral, and changes in cultures/practices alongside a discussion on characteristics and examples of creative knowledge working, importance of creativity, and related abilities and skills. The chapter also provided nuanced and modified versions of co-configuration and epistemic cultures, which were used as methodological approaches to investigating the empirical data.

Notes

1. Levi's twisted to fit advert. (2011). [YouTube]. Available at: http://www.youtube.com/watch?v=-p5aAdr3C8k&feature=related [Last accessed 25th October 2011].
2. 'The history of advertising in quite a few objects: 35 Lucio Fontana's paintings'. Available at: http://www.campaignlive.co.uk/news/1142844/ [Last accessed 25th October 2014].
3. Tibor Kalman (undated). [YouTube]. Available at: https://www.youtube.com/watch?v=cYIAMsXvSTw [Last accessed 5th May 2014].
4. Top 10 Controversial United Colors of Benetton Ads (2012). [Online]. Available at: http://top10buzz.com/top-ten-controversial-united-colors-of-benetton-ads/. [Last accessed 5th May 2014].
5. SMAP [Online]. Available at: http://en.wikipedia.org/wiki/SMAP. [Last accessed 5th May 2014].
6. Based on major media data (such as press, television, radio, cinema, outdoor and Internet). [Online]. Available at: www.asiamediaaccess.com.au/ftimes/adspend/summary.htm. [Last accessed 2nd April 2004] and ZenithOptimedia. [Online]. Available at: http://www.zenithoptimedia.com/zenith/zenithoptimedia-releases-september-2012-advertising-expenditure-forecasts/. [Last accessed 30th December 2012] relating to the two periods—2000 and 2011 respectively. Please note that the currency conversion rates applied to the two years would be different.
7. Although this investigation does not involve cross-country comparison, it may be useful to relate the sector's expenditure to a country with a similar size Gross National Income (GNI). The country with the nearest GNI in 2011 was Poland (US$477.0B), which was ranked twenty-third largest in the world. Countries with smaller GNIs in 2011 included

Norway, Austria, and Denmark. Based on data from the World Bank. [Online]. Available at: http://databank.worldbank.org/databank/download/GNI.pdf. [Last accessed 30 December 2012].

8. Based on data from ZenithOptimedia. [Online]. Available at: http://www.zenithoptimedia.com/zenith/zenithoptimedia-releases-september-2012-advertising-expenditure-forecasts/. [Last accessed 30 December 2012].

9. Based on data from ZenithOptimedia. [Online]. Available at: http://www.zenithoptimedia.com/zenith/zenithoptimedia-releases-september-2012-advertising-expenditure-forecasts/. [Last accessed 30 December 2012].

10. Based on data from ZenithOptimedia. [Online]. Available at: http://www.zenithoptimedia.com/zenith/zenithoptimedia-releases-september-2012-advertising-expenditure-forecasts/. [Last accessed 30 December 2012].

11. Based on data from ZenithOptimedia. [Online]. Available at: www.zenithoptimedia.com/gft/Adspend%20forecasts%20June%202008.pdf. [Last accessed 9th October 2008].

12. Data after 2008 was not easy to access due to the payment restrictions. However, the top ten agencies, according to Wikipedia ([Online]. Available at: http://en.wikipedia.org/wiki/List_of_advertising_agencies_by_revenue. [Last accessed 31 December 2012]), by no means a reliable source, did indicate the lack of movement of the ten largest agencies in comparison to the 2008 data. The one significant movement was in Dentsu, the Japanese agency claiming the top spot. In February 2013, Dentsu would be acquiring the Aegis Group, a British agency, which was featured as the sixth largest agency in 2008.

13. There are two sources of data. The first relates to 2003 from the Advertising Association (2004) *The Marketing Pocket Book 2004*. Henley-on-Thames, England: Advertising Association and World Advertising Research Centre. The second relates to 2012 from Interbrand 'Best Global Brand 2012'. [Online]. Available at: http://www.interbrand.com/en/best-global-brands/2012/downloads.aspx. [Last accessed 30 December 2012]. Interbrand uses a methodology which is based on three components: namely, analyses of the financial performance of the branded products or services, of the role the brand plays in the purchase decision, and of the competitive strength of the brand.

14. Although this study does not involve cross-country comparison, it may be useful to relate the sector's expenditure to a country with a similar size Gross National Income (GNI). Based on data from the World Bank. [Online]. Available at: http://databank.worldbank.org/databank/download/GNI.pdf. [Last assessed 30 December 2012].

8   Information Technology Software I

Contextualization of the Information Technology (IT) Software Sector

This chapter and the next focus on IT software. As mentioned in Chapter 1, this sector was selected because it was found to be one with major characteristics of the knowledge economy, i.e., information technologies.

As explained in the previous two empirical chapters on advertising, these two chapters on IT software will use 'co-configuration' (Victor and Boynton, 1998) and 'epistemic cultures' (Knorr Cetina, 2005a & 2005b) as two methodological approaches to investigating the empirical data (Appendix 1). In addition to these, it will also apply a microsociological stance (Knorr Cetina and Bruegger, 2002a) where 'micro and macro' structures are used to provide contrasts and comparisons of creative knowledge application. Similar to the previous two chapters on advertising, the empirical data gathered is from interviewees comprising of practitioners and academics (Appendix 2 and quotations are denoted by 'SL', e.g., SL 18), relevant external sources, and interdisciplinary theoretical framework to evidence rich and textured exemplars of creative application of knowledge in the IT software sector. By focusing on the creative application of knowledge at three levels: intra-sectoral, inter-sectoral, and the influence of this type of work in operational cultures, this and the following chapters will address the research questions posed in Chapters 1 and 6.

This chapter has three sections. The first provides an introduction to the sector. The second, Micro section, focuses on creative applications of knowledge in IT software. The final section offers a summary.

Micro Descriptions of Creative Applications of Knowledge in the IT Software Sector

This section investigates the micro-analysis of the creative application of knowledge in the IT software sector as it relates to the three revised research questions, the importance of the creative dimension, and the related skills, abilities, and personalities of workers.

Creative Application of Knowledge in the Sector

Creative application of knowledge in this sector is examined in terms of two types of creative jobs: that of a systems software developer and a software programme manager. Each of these jobs provides a description of the creative work, the creative skills, abilities and personalities, and enculturation dimensions such as training, formal and informal education, and ICET. A comparative analysis is featured in the conclusion.

Systems (Software) Developer

The Development Manager of one of the largest global e-security software companies based in the UK provides insights into his company and the role of a software developer:

> The group [of companies] that I run is about content technology. It has a family of products—the highest level is called mine sweeper and underneath there are basically four products. There is the mail sweeper SMTP (Simple Mail Transfer Protocol) and the web suite of products (where you use your browser when searching the Internet, it goes out to request and comes back in and goes onto your web sweeper and the whole web page gets decomposed like Java screen and sits on the boundary of the business. The other is the mail for exchange in which a business going on the Internet has a gateway where the messages and e-mails may be used and this has a boundary. If I send you an e-mail, it sits on this boundary and can be 'sweeped' or checked for viruses. These are the SMTP products and also we have the mail suite for dominos. This is a product, which works with these inside the business, where exchange boxes 'talk' to each other and carry out content checking internally. It is a security system of protecting the data . . .
>
> I think creativity has changed in the light of the knowledge economy where people are more mobile and connected and using the Internet, 3G, and GPS where you can carry out all the applications thus earning money from customers. Thus technology has enabled people to do business more creatively but not necessarily more efficiently. Some companies have spent millions of pounds to install customer relationship management (CRM) systems into their companies and found it was not flexible and so they had to hire consultants to come in to change the system. So it's not always efficient. Each organization has its own system and the software should meet the requirements of that organization, not the organization to the software.
>
> SL18

The above description indicates how a company's activities generate income for software companies. The Executive Deputy Chairman and Chief Technology

Officer of a leading European Application Service Provider, based in the UK, explained how software could generate business:

> Knowledge can be accessed from portable computers, mobile phones and personal digital assistant (PDAs). You can be anywhere and can still be accessed to information. Using IT to generate competitive advantage and companies are outsourcing activities which are not their core activities e.g. we run British Airways financial systems, which are important but not their core activities and with Cisco, we do their back-up where their core business is in designing and selling networking. IT sector is very much part of the knowledge economy.
>
> SL17

The Development Manager went onto explain the activities of his organization in relation to the software functions:

> There are three areas in my organization: software engineers who physically work out the code using a language such as C++, the people who test the software for functionality and it has to be repeatable for reliability, and the last group of software developers, to install the manuals and to maintain it. We have a product road map e.g. in June this year, we will release a version of this and in August, another version etc. and the interphase, we have product managers who collect business requirements which are different to software requirements.
>
> SL18

The description of the roles of a software programme is highly instructive as it provides an understanding of the activities involved in this role. Accompanying these roles are also the abilities and skills that are required and the same interviewee offers further insights:

> We [the e-security software company] cover all aspects of creative work. The first one relates to our company's research such as SMS sweeper, porn sweeper and the second like mine sweeper, with different versions and that's our main profit area. It will come a time when the versions will be outdated and do we go for another version or come up with something new? The skills and abilities for such developmental activities include team working and interpersonal skills. A business opportunity arises and the business requirements become software requirements. In this stage, it involves test engineers to inject quality control in day one, then onto implementation stage, which include test engineers alongside developing it and the 'hardening-up' stage where customers are using the software and then the selling side. In these senses, it's the waterfall scenario if you like or the total quality management system. Anticipation skills are needed. The people we have are diverse—farmer, builder and also graduates. We look for technical skills, thinking skills, and problem solving skills. We use tests

at the interview stage to ascertain knowledge of different disciplines and on their curriculum vitae; we look at the experiences and contacts such as word of mouth and recruitment agencies. The skills such as team working are about communication, honesty where software engineers need to be realistic in their abilities to complete the job, their estimate in the time required to do it and the problems if any arising where they need to inform the project manager. We have a 'no blame' culture, it's about what you learn and move people out if they are not performing. The skills with research, they need to be more creative and not necessarily just problem solvers but more focused on object oriented and behavior i.e. how does the component/object behave and if we neglect any of these things, then we have problems with the software in terms of functionality/procedural, behavior and abstract. Also, they require anticipatory imagination for example this is how a mine sweeper works and having a prototype and picking up an SMTP and dropping an antivirus software (AV) into it and the whole decomposition engine evolves—that's how we end up with ideas and products. We need people to have ideas.

SL18

The above descriptions of the various roles of a software developer/engineer offer a better understanding of the creative knowledge work in this sector. A creative application of knowledge is in the generation of ideas. Having the ability to anticipate users' desires, or an anticipatory imagination, is important as a systems developer can use technical and cultural knowledge to produce a more efficient/user-friendly software, which in words of the interviewee is 'seamless.' A systems developer intuits what users desire as explained by Reich's (2001) in his description of the "shrink" creative worker.

In addition to the above, using the software programmers at Microsoft as illustrative of the roles of this group of creative workers might also be useful. They include: determining the vision for new features, designing the features, allocating project resources, building the features, testing the features, and preparing the product for shipping (Cusumano and Selby, 1997, p. 83). Software developers need to ascertain and evaluate what each feature seeks to accomplish and also to imagine how users engage with the software. This might be called anticipatory imagination where the developer anticipates what and how the user would find engaging and applies this knowledge to enhance the software's user-friendliness and applicability. The design features consist of understanding the computer instructions or algorithms necessary to carry out the required tasks and an understanding of the compatibility with other features and products (such as Microsoft Word) (Cusumano and Selby, 1997, p. 83). In terms of project resource allocation, the duration of this programming task must be ascertained and adhered to or else the financial viability, marketability, and dependability of the project and corporate image might be compromised. This process is done in consultation with the relevant team and project manager on the basis of previous working experience. The function of features focuses on coding and reviewing code with other developers and programme managers where potential issues relating to size of memory, dependency of a code on specific hardware processors, and 'zero-defect programming' are discussed. The last issue relates to the "synch-and-stabilize process that relies on daily product builds, milestone stabilizations, and daily testing as well as debugging" (Cusumano and Selby, 1997, p. 84). The next role is the testing of the software code where developers and testers work together to iron out bugs in the code. This is done on a daily basis while asking users for feedback and incorporating their views into the coding (Cusumano and Selby, 1997, p. 84). The last stage relates to the preparation of product delivery. The focus is to refrain from making major changes to the code and to eliminate bugs through intensive testing. The connection between the developer and users is important to the commercial viability of the product.

Technical knowledge is relevant in this highly specialized field. Comments by practitioners (e.g., the Senior Manager of a Japanese software company [SL23], the Programme Development Manager of one of the largest global UK based e-security software companies [SL18]), and academics (at universities of Singapore [SL31] and Tokyo [SL26]) indicated that Java and C++ were the most relevant languages. This is critical because a highly portable computer language is important. The Institute for the Management of Information Systems (IMIS) in the UK listed the top ten software languages in recruitment advertising as Java, C++, Internet General, Unix, SQL, Windows NT, Oracle, Visual Basic, HTML and C (Virgo, 2001). In a report by Dench (1998), the top ten technical skills were C, C++. Visual Basic, Object Oriented programming Java, Unix, Oracle, networking, including local area networking (LAN), data communications, and multimedia. This type of knowledge is explicit and discipline-related and acquired through formal education such as at a university, a professional course, or training whilst working.

The other type of knowledge is less explicit and more tacit and acquired in less formal circumstances. Bill Gates's views (BBC, 2007) on what type of knowledge is necessary to succeed as a software programmer might be said to be highly relevant here. However, this example has to be cited with caution (as a software developer) because he is one of the luminaries and investigation does not focus on unique and exceptional talents. He suggested that one should have an ongoing passion for learning, read widely on a broad range of subjects, find information that is of interest to oneself, and be curious about the world (BBC, 2007). This ability to be curious about the surrounding world and be a general sponge has resonance with creative workers in the advertising sector. This openness to life experiences may be illustrated by a professor at a university in Tokyo (SL26). He was involved in research with a Japanese company before entering academia and held professorial chairs in the US HEIs, as well as establishing a consultancy practice working with start-up venture companies in the Silicon Valley. He also was on the panel of judges for a non-IT award: the prestigious Nikkei BP Advertising Award. He advocated, along with other interviewees, a wider experience and knowhow to IT software working:

> The skills needed are the ability to handle UNIX software, deep understanding of semi-conductor, physics for circuits. These require

multi-disciplinary knowledge. In my industry, there are different levels starting from process engineers (having the ability to process etc. and deposit software into a system), devise engineers (the ability to amalgamate the unit technologies to make a transistor or beta connections), design, system, software and assembly engineers.

. . . creativity also involves taking pleasure in experiencing new things, perhaps in the genes for example, going to a cafeteria at your place of work or university and ordering different things every day or trying new restaurants which are pleasurable to them. We also need motivation and curiosity. In terms of development, one has to work within the law of solids (as theoretical frameworks), one has to have motivation and deep knowledge and expertise in more than one discipline. In the level of jobs of being knowledgeable in physics (first level), one does not require skills or in communication or curiosity unlike the higher level jobs but they require more self-discipline. What is a good business model or what is the application of this technology at the higher levels require good communication skills. The other aspect of creativity [in relation to creative knowledge work] include awareness and openness to things such as experiencing happiness, how to keep a city clean rather than constructing a large building in a desert. So we need abilities like reliability, attention to details and an aesthetic sense. Business acumen is also preferable.

SL26

There appears to be an aesthetic sensibility (as described by Lash and Urry (1994)) in the form of elegance and intelligibility (MacLennan, 2008) of technical expression. This aesthetic sensibility may not be understood by the user but it may be appreciated by fellow software programmers. The professor at a Tokyo university (SL27) described the creative act of writing software as requiring a "power of expression." This form of creative knowledge application offers an example of how work contributes to changing the culture or practice when aesthetic sensibility is applied to a highly technical discipline, especially in relation to the eventual production of and application by users of the software products. In addition, this form of creative knowledge work, power of expression, offers insights into the possible technical and emotional connections between the producers (software developers) and those with such technical insights. Nerland (2008, p. 60) described this aesthetic and technical combination as the "ability to see the unfulfilled potential inherent in the technological scene."

Related to the aesthetic sensibility is 'sensitivity,' which interviewees mentioned as part of the arsenal of skills and abilities for creative knowledge workers in this sector. Here are three perspectives of sensitivity from three academics respectively:

Sensitivity is like an antenna and if we can hear it differently and sharply focus on it for 24 hours, we can quickly respond."

SL24

"how successful we are is dependent on how well we have learnt about the external environment which is anything outside ourselves. So we need to put ourselves into the minds of others in order to learn and utilize the experience for the future—that is a soft skill. This can mean getting into the language of the person, knowing his/her thought processes, comforts and fears and so I have to effectively assume the personality of that person I am engaging with.

SL28

We also need to develop such kinds of sensitivity. It also includes the construction of strategies, which are related to the use of technology in the real world and sensitivity to the real world.

SL25

The description of the sensitivity skill as 'an antennae' has strong resonance with the phrases "a general sponge" and "social chameleon" and "in tune with the zeitgeist" applied by the interviewees in the previous two empirical chapters on advertising. It is the awareness of the environment (such as the cultural, physical, emotional, political, and physical) by the creative knowledge worker and how this may be used in relation to her/his activities, which contribute towards the eventual creation and production of a product or service such as software or video game in this sector.

Also as indicated above, software programmers/developers collaborate with other experts and soft skills such as team working and interpersonal skills are useful. Included in this approach for collaboration is the ability to be able to communicate effectively.

Having the relevant technical knowledge and to a lesser degree, cultural knowledge is important with regard to creative knowledge work for a systems developer because it relies on knowledge applied creatively through problem solving, creation of ideas, anticipatory imagination, power of expression, and sensitivity.

(Software) Programme Manager

Unlike a systems software developer discussed above, a software programme manager has other functions. A researcher with a Japanese company specializing in electronics noted:

For [software] managers, give them incentives so as to make them hungry. The best way is to throw them into a risky field, which is unknown to the managers and specify this field to them. The choice of the field should be based on your deep and accumulated experiences and make them tackle problems as specifically as possible. One should not always look for large or significant difference and one should recognize the small differences instead.

SL24

The above description implies that a software programme manager should lead the project and coordinate a project bearing the specific issue in mind. Bruce Ryan, a programme manager at the Microsoft software company, described his role as:

> The program manager is a leader, facilitator, and coordinator, but is *not* the boss.
>
> (Ryan interview, cited in Cusumano and Selby, 1997, p. 77)

This leads on to the question how does a programme manager perform all of these roles of leader, facilitator, and coordinator, concomitantly? Knowledge is important in creative knowledge working in this technical sector, but the individual must also have technological knowhow in the relevant software language such as Java and C++ so that the complexities of issues in the development aspects can be explained to software developers/programmers. Indeed, the indication of software languages was mentioned in the previous creative job by interviewees in the investigation.

Another interviewee, a professor at a university in Tokyo, offered the following descriptions of a programme manager:

> A planner or manager who has good knowledge of technology who proposes new models of business or product improvements where the ideas originate from the person requires commercial vision and acumen and the abilities to lead a team from start to finish. So she/he proposes, implements and completes the project. An example is Ms Mari Matsunaga, the product manager of the second generation of mobile phones who was recruited to join NTT DoCoMo [mobile company in Japan]. This generation of mobile phones uses e-mail, text messages and Internet etc. Initially, it was not seen as a viable idea because the display of text messages on the tiny screen was rather limited. The technology was not very advanced.
>
> SL27

The eventual fruition of the mobile phone described above offers insights into how software activities may be applied in an inter-sectoral manner. The description also offers some insights into the activities of a manager such as commercial vision, acumen, and leadership skills. As a facilitator and coordinator, the programme manager needs to have knowledge of the team so that they perform to the best of their ability. This requires excellent interpersonal skills. The manager is a coordinator and has to liaise with several related parties including the organization's executives to establish the vision that will inform the design of the software.

Vision can only be created by application of knowledge, which may be technical, past job experiences, or culture-related, and it should be communicated clearly to the team of developers and marketing team and others. It should be done in a way that convinces the team that the vision has positive, realistic achievable outcomes, and is what consumers or users want. To convey this vision, leadership abilities are necessary (discussed in Chapter 4 by Sternberg et al. [2004, p. 146]), and include the ability to convince workers of the relevance of it, the ability to motivate them to both implement and execute it efficiently.

Another team may be software developers who are responsible for writing the software. The third team are software testers who are responsible for ironing out any bugs that could disrupt the functioning of the software. Others teams include marketing who are responsible for advertising and distributing to users. The talents required by the coordinator of all of this includes the ability to communicate technical and non-technical aspects of the intended product to all teams and if necessary re-framing it in a language that is accessible. This collaborative approach to working and communicating with team members is explained by SL18:

> There are some software engineers who are very good at turning the business requirement into software for example more throughput for messages but how do you quantify the amount of messages as some messages are short and others lengthier? Also there is the architecture. Some [software] engineers are good at doing design work at the high end—say a 6–9 month cycle. Other engineers are happier on a shorter cycle like a two-week piece of work such as the 'patches' i.e. maintenance. The key thing is to understand, as a manager, the skill sets of these engineers and meet the aspirations of the staff together with the reality of the business environment. So, one as a manager needs to motivate these engineers. Software and testing engineers are not just there for the money but also it's about their technical skill set and they also want to be team and project leaders.
>
> SL18

Thus, communication abilities of an accurate and detailed nature are important. A programme manager's 'sensitivities' to the needs of the teams, the project requirements, and the end users are important. The close workings of the programme manager with his/her developers and testers are crucial in creating software that not only fits the specifications but also meets the needs of the users; the latter point drives the former. The combinations that are essential in the multi-dimensional roles of a programme manager include: an appropriate vision and the ability to convey, convince, and motivate the team to write and deliver the software to a deadline with the required functions/features wanted by users. Leaders can enable others, using their knowledge and ability to communicate. SL17 provided these specific insights:

> The ideas need to be weighted and an organization cannot cope with 50 ideas but perhaps they need to be prioritised not based on the Chairman's idea but on a scientific approach using weighting factors. These can be taught like organizational skills. One needs to break down barriers in an organization to allow people to articulate their ideas. Some ideas may not be useful but this is part of the game. On the communication side, the skills

needed are the ability to listen as in any meeting, someone would want to dominate a meeting thus need a chair to keep a balance, to be open minded when receiving an idea which may be a silly idea but may trigger a better one, ability to take other ideas as better than your own and collectively we can do something. Thus an organization needs to have a balance of skills.

SL17

Activities of creative knowledge application include a) using knowledge to generate ideas, b) an anticipatory imagination of the needs and wants of the users, c) sensitivity to the requirements and needs of stakeholders, d) vision of the programme manager, and e) knowledge of the users' interests. All of these combined can lead to commercially successful production.

Besides ideas and anticipatory imagination, the next creative application is problem solving, which is rooted in the individual's own knowledge. Insights are offered by a partner of a software development and consultancy company in Singapore with operations in Asia and New Zealand:

> Creativity depends on how we view problems, and how do we creatively solve them. Too often, creativity is concentrated on the solving of problems. Perhaps, the more interesting part of creativity is viewing problems. Problem solving could be learnt through experience like these are the best practices and role models etc. In fact the world of consulting could be praised or blamed because we are taking solutions and mapping to problems telling our customers these are the good solutions. How do we come to this initial conclusion that this is the best solution to this problem? I am not sure it is creativity or as mundane as a database access! I am not sure of this part but if we call the matching of solutions to problems as creative thinking, then one can learn a lot of it through experience, sharing and accessing knowledge. The most difficult is to integrate the problem—are you able to transform it to another problem? This will give you a lot of opportunities to solve in an impactful way. That I am not sure if there are techniques to teach people—to me it just clicks.
>
> SL28

Problem solving on the basis of the above requires technical, past job experience as well as creativity. This example illustrates a combination of Gardner's (1999) logical-mathematical and spatial intelligences. This is because a software programme manager needs to apply logic, to seek and solve technical problems, but also have the ability to have spatial (technical) awareness to view it from different perspectives.

Relating to this is a focus and concentration for innovation. SL24 explained the process and his passion as follows:

> Concentration with deep long time thinking on solving existing problems and making it as specific as possible are necessary. It allows you to create

a 'small' difference. Don't stop thinking even if the difference is short of big advantages and high quality. Accumulated small differences will eventually create innovations. Concentration is also needed and so is job satisfaction. In my case, using my ideas in the products is my biggest satisfaction. Thus one has to be dedicated.

You can create a big difference when you are suffering from troubles involved in your products because the problems are deeply grasped. You need to envision the possible problems in the future and make the difference by analogy using past but similar technologies. When you create an idea, you need to check if it is relevant in terms of applicability. Successful presentations or proposals are effective to create a trend by convincing others.

SL24

With regard to knowledge and qualifications, a programme manager would require a technical undergraduate degree at the very minimum. Some managers have arts and humanities-related degrees or in business, but these must enable them to understand basic technical issues. They do not need to be versed in programming though some do carry out some degree of it and they must have a strong knowledge and interest in design and software programming.

Comparison of the Two Creative Jobs on Knowledge Application

This final part offers a comparative analysis of the two creative jobs in terms of their creative application of knowledge, the creative skills and talents required, and personalities needed in relation to the theoretical framework.

The two creative IT software roles of a software programme/developer and a software programme manager offer insights into how knowledge is applied creatively. Both are centred on creating software for application such as Word and Excel and for entertainment such as Grand Theft Auto IV and World of Warcraft video games.

They have similarities, including knowledge of: technical nature in software, team members in more than one discipline, collaboration, and creative application. Creative application of knowledge involved problem solving, ideas, anticipatory imagination, 'power of expression' and aesthetic sensibilities, and 'sensitivity.'

The two software workers require technical knowledge related to software. In the case of a software programmer, knowledge of a software language such as Java and C++ is critical to write software. This was indicated by some of the interviewees and writers such as Dench (1998) and Virgo (2001). However, the degree of technical expertise may be less for a programme manager, as only knowledge of the language is necessary to understand the issues for communicating with the team of developers and testers. This technical aspect requires formal qualifications and training.

Specific insights by the interviewee who was an academic at a university in London explained this technical training and knowledge base in comparison with those trained at the Royal College of Art, with greater emphasis on the aesthetic side of design:

> I start off by saying that you can go to the Royal College of Art where they are using a different sort of skill and placing much more weight on creativity and less on technology. I think you see a different sort of product. This product can be very successful in the cultural world and it contributes to the knowledge economy. It's a different world to the xxx product. The xxx product is based much more on science and technology and you rely on this huge knowledge base, which the graduates and researchers have at their disposal to exploit, and turned into application. In many cases these applications are more evolutionary than real creativity.
>
> SL21

Knowledge of other disciplines may also be required as corroborated by a professor at a higher education institution in Tokyo with experiences in Silicon Valley and a professorship in the US. He explained:

> Until ten years ago, there was only one level. Now there are 2/3 levels of jobs, which are concerned, not with the knowledge of physics (which is unchangeable) but changeable laws/systems which may impact on society by changing people's attitudes. What is needed now is deep knowledge in at least three levels and so an IT developer needs to be multi-disciplined.
>
> SL26

In certain software areas such as entertainment (e.g., gaming) and IT applications, knowledge of cultural trends is relevant as these require a knowledge and insight into what users desire and want. The developments in technologies provide greater scope for interaction between software knowledge workers and users. The next chapter on ICET, which examines the closer workings between producers and users, will analyze this further.

Bill Gates (BBC, 2007, p. 1) suggested that a successful programmer needed to be a general sponge of the past and present cultural trends. Part of this knowledge acquisition requires curiosity of the world as well as cultural events via text, Internet, experiences, etc.

Another area of commonality between the two knowledge workers is collaborative working. It forms one of the two dimensions in the conceptual framework (discussed in Chapter 5) as outlined by Csikszentmihalyi (1988), Nonaka and Takeuchi (1995) and von Hippel (2006).

Having the right team chemistry is important and Sawyer noted:

> Conflict keeps the group from falling into the groupthink trap. But conflict is difficult to manage productively because it can easily spiral into

destructive interpersonal attacks that interfere with creativity. Diversity enhances performance only when the group flow factors are present, including some degree of shared knowledge; a culture of close listening and open communication; a focus on well-defined goals; autonomy, fairness, and equal participation.

(Sawyer, 2007, p. 71)

The shared knowledge, close communication involving technical knowledge, defined goals, and participation were all elements mentioned by interviewees such as the Executive Deputy Chairman and Chief Technology Officer (SL17), the Development Manager (SL18), and the professor at a Japanese university (SL27).

Knowledge of team members is useful and critical abilities, as discussed by Csikszentmihalyi (1988), Gardner (1999) and Reich (2001) included communicating, team working, listening, motivating a team, and setting a common goal and deadline. Gardner (1999) used interpersonal and intrapersonal intelligences to explain the abilities for this style of working. The programme manager's abilities in facilitating and coordinating the project are essential soft skills.

Common to the two jobs are creative application of knowledge. These include problem solving, generating ideas, applying anticipatory imagination, using power of expression and aesthetic sensibilities, and sensitivity. Problem solving was explained by an interviewee, a researcher at a Japanese company, in the previous section. He also included passion alongside hard work, focus, and concentration. Reich's (2001) creative workers had problem solving as part of their personalities. In this sector, a software creative knowledge worker creates and designs a new product by anticipating users' desires.

Generating ideas is highly significant in these creative roles. This includes developing specific functions for an existing software. The space for creativity exists beyond problem solving in this highly technical and logical sector. It requires the software developer's "ability to see the unfulfilled potential inherent in the technological scene." This was mentioned by Nerland (2008, p. 60) and also the software development manager interviewed and noted earlier.

This creative approach involves Gardner's (1999) notion of creativity by asking new questions and doing something novel. Linking ideas to problem solving is another creative application for a programme manager as advocated by Fine (Cusumano and Selby, 1997) in the previous section. Fine mentioned that a creative programme manager must have an overview of the problem and be able to view it from several perspectives. This will enable a solution. Technical knowhow and previous job experiences are relevant in the use of "sapient tacit knowledge" as mentioned by Guile (2006, p. 362). Relating to the theoretical framework, this approach evokes Gardner's (1999) logical-mathematical and spatial intelligences.

Another ability is anticipatory imagination. This means that both a software developer and manager must be able to empathize with users of the software. Specific insights about this by SL28 are:

Yes, at the end of the day, how successful we are as a software programmer is dependent on how well we have learnt about the external environment which is anything outside ourselves. So we need to put ourselves into the minds of others in order to learn and utilize the experience for the future—that is a soft skill. This can mean getting into the language of the person, thought process, comforts and fears of the person. So I have to effectively assume the personality of that person/user I am engaging with.

SL28

The ability to anticipate the imagination of the user requires knowledge of the world. This creative approach is similar to Reich's "geek" (2001, p. 49) who intuits the user's needs.

The next commonality between the two creative roles relates to what one interviewee calls 'the power of expression.' This comment was made by a professor at a Japanese university (SL27). This notion was elaborated earlier by Hanson at MIT and a participant of the open software community (Linux) as involving an aesthetic expression and wanting others "to share the beauty of what they have found" (von Hippel, 2006, p. 124). It was discussed by Lash and Urry (1994) who noted that the IT software industry had this in common with culture industries.

The final commonality relates to 'sensitivity' or an ability to take into account the needs of the users/consumers, workers, in relation to the specifications of the project. This was described by SL24, SL25, and SL28 as relevant and significant in the eventual execution of a targeted software project.

The next part relates to differences between the two jobs. Bruce Ryan (Cusumano and Selby, 1997, p. 77) at Microsoft captures these differences in his description of the role of a programme manager, as "a leader, facilitator and coordinator, but is *not* the boss."

A software development manager requires a vision of the software including other leadership qualities. These creative approaches require knowledge of the team. The application of a team's knowledge is different for a programme manager compared to that of a systems programmer. The former persuades and convinces the team of the vision and motivates them to create software. The latter presents ideas, communicates, and collaborates with the team to a successful end. Gardner's (1999) two personal intelligences, i.e., inter- and intrapersonal are useful to understand this.

These skills must also be viewed alongside the others mentioned above. A programme manager, unlike a programme developer, needs a strong interest in design issues and software programming with the ability to sell, convince, and motivate people to implement the vision.

Summary

This chapter provided rich descriptions of creative knowledge working in two roles: systems developer and programme manager that are linked to the theoretical framework. It argued on the basis of empirical evidence that knowledge in this creative sector focused on technical knowledge of a discipline-related variety, which drives creative approaches.

9 Information Technology Software II

Introduction

This second chapter on IT software discusses the micro and macro dimensions of creative knowledge work, identified as themes in the theoretical chapters. The introduction section in the previous chapter on the two methodological approaches of 'co-configuration' (Victor and Boynton, 1998) and 'epistemic cultures' (Knorr Cetina, 2005a and 2005b) and the microsociology methodological approach (Knorr Cetina and Bruegger, 2002a) apply here. Following the introduction, this chapter has the following sections: micro dimensions of creative applications of knowledge in the IT software sector, its macro descriptions, and observations and insights.

Micro Dimensions of Creative Applications of Knowledge in the IT Software Sector

This section is divided into four parts: namely, significance of ICET, closer working between producers and users, enculturation processes of this type of work, and a summary.

Significance of ICET and the IT Software Sector

Descriptions of the roles of the two creative knowledge workers in the previous chapter showed that ICET is a significant element in IT software. Knowledge of IT software such as C++ is essential for a systems developer whereas the systems manager requires a technical understanding of the software to communicate with the team but not necessarily to write the programme. In addition, an aesthetic dimension is also needed.

A professor at an English university with training in engineering and a specialization in software gave his insights on the knowledge economy:

> It is based on information—the manipulation and presentation of information. These include industries like banking, management consultancy

and even companies like IBM is moving from a manufacturing hardware base to one of offering a service.

SL20

The above offers a view of the application of knowledge in a service-oriented economy with manufacturing industries using knowledge to create cutting edge tangible products. This is supported by a sophisticated IT base, which permeates all facets, and both on corporate and personal dimensions.

The Executive Deputy Chairman and Chief Technology Officer and co-founder of a software company in England offered his views on creativity and the IT software sector:

> I've always thought creativity is important . . . There is a greater willingness to recognize that there is a role for creativity in organizations and there are now computer tools to harness your thoughts to become more creative e.g. mind mapping and outlines. It is becoming easier to be creative especially with access to information in the Internet where you may have an idea and surf the Internet and follow up the link and settle on a lot of ideas, which may spark off other ideas . . . There are three aspects to software and creativity. One is the organizational tools to help you to organize ideas etc. The second is that the Internet is a tremendous source of ideas especially websites. The third is that computers enable you to model things so one can build say a power station on a computer, financial modeling looking at trends with what if scenarios. Thus there are now tools to help us, wider resources and machines to help us to verify our ideas.

SL17

The Internet may be a source of information and software can be used as a tool to store and organize it and to model complex activities with varying scenarios. Software can enhance the capabilities and complexities of creative knowledge work. One such activity of an inter-sectoral working was illustrated by a professor of computing at a London university:

> The next generation of scientific infrastructure will be network computers in collaborative work with other scientists over the web using computers. Our job is to develop software to help that happen, which is developing software for the scientific world over different disciplines e.g. medicines, physics etc. It is the first government initiative, which spans all the research councils. What is perceived is that some of the software will be generic e.g. methods of connecting computers together, networking i.e. the basic software structure—the grid. The rationale of the government is that there is a high degree of commonality between scientific disciplines e.g. modeling in environmental sciences and in physics.

SL19

He went on to describe the different levels of work:

> "Currently, a lot of the scientific work is computationally based, which involves a lot of scientists from different disciplines like chemists, engineers etc. Thus a lot of the time the attention is on low level work whereas a lot of e-science work is to automate that and to choose the appropriate method—appropriate computer, relevant modeling method and present the results in a very visual manner. Once the level of abstraction is raised then one can begin to start to correlate the different sources of data. The scientists can then focus much more on the hypothesis that generates and the serendipitous associations of the data and work more at a creative level.
>
> SL19

For the professor, IT software offers a way to alleviate the lower level work such as computational activities in order that the workers could focus on higher level work such as analysis and associations arising from data. Software offers more time and space to workers to utilize their creativity in higher level work.

The application of IT software in work provides greater opportunities for creative knowledge workers to use their knowledge and creativity. Some of the interviewees offered inter-sectoral examples of new ways of working whether on generic or specific levels. The first was from an academic at an English university (SL21). The second was from a professor at a Japanese university (SL27), and the third was a Managing Director of a computer company in Singapore (SL28).

> Undoubtedly, the whole of the telecom industry has been a product of much more powerful information technology. I was a little bit surprised to discover that teletex software is a logical product and so the people who built those things are primarily software people. Standard software and computer science techniques with the new particular device/environment—writing programme to mobile phones or to control the routing of the messages or writing programmes to exchanges etc. are all software. It is less concern with competent picture of knowledge. It is IT—you only move across to find the same sort of people who provide new web services or helping you to problem solve organizational problems.
>
> SL21

> There are jobs that are related to the knowledge economy. These can include webpage designing, which require different ways of thinking and varies disciplinary knowledge. The postgraduate qualifications are not valued in industry and in government ministries [in Japan] and these postgraduates will become researchers.
>
> SL27

More jobs exist now that are knowledge based and we are not talking about chief knowledge officers [CKO], which is just a label but jobs to do with people and involved in intelligence—business intelligence—where it looks at market trends, competition, product positioning and development. Companies find that they have shorter time to market their services and products as information, which can be so persuasive. Whatever you think was useful and in no time, it would be information to your competitors. With equal access to information then, what is your edge? In the past, knowledge is power and it made a lot of sense, but now, what is next? It has to be something to do with how well you are able to process or transform knowledge in your head to create some insights that is unique to that business. There should be a lot more attention to not just the roles of information officers, which actually should be obsolete as information is readily available. There should be investment in people who could be called 'thought leaders.' If we do not invest in this, then we are forever following some trends. Perhaps, CKOs could be renamed Chief Information Officers (CIOs).

SL28

The above descriptions of new areas of work require multi-disciplinary knowhow as well as analytical skills. Technological improvements using IT software offer greater opportunities for creative workers to utilize their creative skills towards the eventual production of innovative products/services such as the second generation of mobile phones resulting from ideas/concepts. The Managing Director of a computer company based in Singapore offered some insights as to the capabilities of some of the new roles:

> The roles in these new areas of work have to do with being unconventional—in thinking, ability to question what is possible. It is a cliché to say 'think out of a box,' but it is easier said than done. One has to have the discipline to continually stretch the boundaries of the possibilities and to have the ability to paint the scenario of the future. It is not a dreaming job but the ability to piece together scenarios for the future and others can use these to come up with something constructive. It has to be a vision, which on the one hand, it breaks away from what is possible today and on the other, it is actionable [anticipatory imagination]. I ask people to think of the future and question—does it have to be this way? One can benefit through exposure to certain tools and things or from training. It is a discipline which has to be exercised continuously.

SL28

These capabilities and knowledge offer additional insights to those discussed in the earlier roles of IT software designing and managing where anticipatory imagining, asking and seeking the relevant questions, and solving the problems were required.

As indicated in the previous empirical chapter and from a methodological approach of 'co-configuration' (Victor and Boynton, 1998), there are new technological developments and a greater connection between users and producers (Victor and Boynton, 1998; Quah, 2002; von Hippel, 2006). These include platforms such as mobile phones, tablets (e.g., iPad), Internet television (e.g., 4oD and iPlayer), entertainment gaming with greater human interaction (e.g., Kinect games and World of Warcraft online game), 'modding' (where rules of the game can be modified) games (e.g., Quake and Half-Life), and software applications (e.g., Apps). These connections between producers (of video games) and users offer closer interactions in terms of the emotional attachments with the product. They may be in the form of a user with the product or between users in the same video game, or between them collectively with the game, where in some games such as Half-Life, the users have input in the eventual outcome. These interactions offer a more nuanced connection between producers and users via the video games, where emotional connections are created directly between users and product and indirectly between users and producer (from the branding point of view as discussed in the previous chapter).

This trend of connecting users and producers and between users calls for a different approach to creative knowledge working for software workers. Knowledge is not restricted to technology-related knowledge. These workers require cultural knowledge (being a general sponge) as well as knowledge of more than one discipline as mentioned by a professor of a university in Tokyo (SL26). With this broadening out of knowledge base, a creative knowledge worker in software needs to focus on aesthetic sensibilities in relation to taste and beauty of the programmers, but also users. These aesthetics sensibilities as advocated by Lash and Urry (1994) and Reich (2001) refer to the storyline of a modding game, and visual imagery, symbols, and signs of an App. Functionality is important but an aesthetic eye is important, too.

From the methodological approach of 'epistemic cultures,' the knowledge generated, circulated, and used by the software community was supported by ICET. This was identified by Knorr Cetina (2005b) in her study of foreign exchange markets. However, there are differences between the IT software form of epistemic culture and Knorr Cetina's foreign exchange markets. These are the impact of ICET on the work of creative knowledge workers, impact on the job market, creativity, and relevance to everyday activities. From the empirical evidence in this section, ICET can be said to be an organizational tool, a source of ideas (such as the Internet), and a means of modelling a concept (as evidenced by SL 17). ICET can also be used in inter-sectoral activities such as software for cross-disciplinary applications (as evidenced by SL 19). These technological developments enable creative knowledge workers (such as software developers) to spend more time away from automated activities and focus more on complex activities such as data analysis (SL19). In effect, ICET changes the way creative knowledge workers carry out their activities. From the perspective of the job market, technological developments offer new varieties of jobs such as webpage designers (as identified by SL 27) and 'thought leaders' (SL28).

In terms of creativity this is different from Knorr Cetina's foreign exchange market users, because it is focused on advanced technologies allowing creative knowledge workers more time to concentrate on the creative aspects of their work due to increased automation and supportive applications such as modelling. Creativity, in a sense, becomes more intensified for creative applications. As evidenced in the previous section, these applications include: anticipatory imagination, seeking and asking relevant questions, solving problems and aesthetic sensibilities, and sensitivity. Lastly, IT software as evidenced in digital products such as mobile phones, laptops, and entertainment products are part of the professional and personal landscape. Without software, according to Hoch, Roeding, Purkert and Lindner (1999), there would be no fax, email, and business voice mail. In terms of cross-industrial implications, software also controlled nuclear power plants, recognized customer purchasing patterns, enabled stock trading, facilitated banking systems/cell phone structures, and enabled oil exploration.

In short, 'software is pure knowledge in codified form which drives and enables today's economy' (Hoch et al., 1999, p. 7). These factors of IT software culture are different and broader than Knorr Cetina's (2005b) foreign exchange market 'epistemic culture.'

Closer Working between Producers and Users in the Sector

This section explores the relationships between producers and users, where information enabled the design and creation of innovative products and services to a targeted consumer base. There are several observations: the perceptions of data in relation to its potential uses; the relationships with the science community, businesses, and the wider societal stakeholders; the possibility of its application in changing the culture of an organization and its business activities; and the means to measure such activities.

Interviewees such as SL17 and SL18 discussed the relevance of IT software in relation to the financial activities of their organizations and their clients. Interviewee SL18 noted:

> So the use of IT [software] is not the be all and end all but a way of doing business, like a bank, it is a way of doing business. Knowledge is the management speak of a new label. It used to be called data mining or data warehousing. Our customer list is worth a fortune. The data in companies is static like personnel data and you need tools to perform analysis such as 'information scanning' with other databases such as emails in order to extract useful information. So, I see knowledge as information about customers and how the way you do business.
>
> SL18

The above illustrates a clear relationship between company activities and client portfolio from the perspective of business and knowledge creation from the application of IT software. It offers an example of IT software practices, which goes beyond its business application to noting how it changed the way in which the security software company viewed its business potential and how its clients recognized the potential of data. This realization could impact its activities.

Other interviewees viewed the applications of IT software in wider terms:

> Going back to your observation about the belief that the technologies pro-
> duced here [development of software for the scientific world over differ-
> ent disciplines by researchers at xxx] will provide technology for the next
> generation in this knowledge economy, there is a very strong convergence
> going on in the way the science community is using computers and the
> way society and businesses are using computers. It will not be a one-way
> traffic but both ways. The next generation of web is semantics web that
> is it will be more intelligent and will not be a static database and differ-
> ent computers looking at a piece of information like an airline ticket will
> understand the information and be able to find say the cheapest fare. The
> other way it is going is it might offer services for example find the best
> pension to suit my circumstances thus requiring the computer to carry
> out computation and sophisticated optimization. This might be the next
> generation of the knowledge economy.
>
> SL19

> Regarding Japan, it was very strong in manufacturing and most of the
> Japanese industries have been shifting from manufacturing to knowledge/
> information technology based industries. This is because, you know, the
> technology has moved and can easily be moved from country to country
> (Asian countries has been advancing rapidly in manufacturing and tech-
> nology) and more value added technology is very important and crucial
> for survival. Moreover, only some technology can be easily moved from
> country to country. Japan has to create pure knowledge, which is new
> and recently created and technology to survive. How can we create new
> technologies? We need to know the trend of the market. If we create new
> knowledge based on the leading countries and companies to the needs of
> the people (nationally and globally) that is pure knowledge (the need to
> humanize the technology and knowledge in terms of using technology
> and knowledge for the benefit of mankind). I think this is the knowledge
> economy.
>
> SL25

The above interviewee, a professor at a university in Japan (SL25) with over four hundred patents in his name and a chief contributor in the field of Auton-omous Decentralized Systems (ADS) (maintainable distributed computer sys-tems), provided a global perspective that involved the 'benefit of mankind.' This is an example of a change in practice in the IT software sector which has a wider application beyond its sector. The professor at English university (SL19) saw IT software in more specific terms such as the functionality of software. In both cases, IT software was perceived as a positive global contribution rather than just a closer relationship between producer and user. SL25 gave a more specific illustration by citing stakeholders at his university:

> I am collaborating with four HEIs, engineers, customers, industry, manufacturers and government of course, we need government financial support to achieve a holistic system using technology. The four HEIs are Tokyo University of Technology, Hitotsubashi (famous for economics and law), Tokyo Medical and Dental University of Tokyo, and Tokyo Hurandang University offering an intellectual property course (using Hitotsubashi law expertise) for undergraduates, as one university cannot cover all the disciplines. Undergraduate students are education based and graduate students are research based. Even now the undergraduates we have to change the teaching methods—like case studies.
>
> SL25

Another example of closer collaboration was offered by a Japanese professor (SL26) when he was asked to be on a panel of judges in the Nikkei BP Advertising Award. This is an example of the inter-sectoral activity between the IT software and advertising sectors.

This perspective of the knowledge economy focuses on the potential creative uses of knowledge and the multiple uses of technologies and new knowledge for the benefit of mankind. However, it implies a more balanced view of potential conflicts such as displacements of resources (both human, physical, and environmental) in a knowledge society.

The next example relates to both an inter-sectoral approach to creative knowledge working as well change in practices of an organization. Here, a train operator in Tokyo, Japan. The creator of the Autonomous Decentralized System (ADS), is in the field of reliable and maintainable distributed computer systems and its applications include the Shinkansen (Bullet train), the Tokyo Metropolitan railway information and control system and the Kawasaki steel production system, was the professor at a Japanese university (SL25). His account of the incorporation of the ADS system to the Japan Railway Company is mentioned below:

> One application is with the Japan Railway Company (JR) where its main business was to transport people. The company is now a large IT company and with a huge amount of computers, they are producing software. They recently started the IC card (rail card using IC chip). The money is registered on the card (like how credit cards are used in Japan, with topped up credits first rather than in the UK, purchases are paid at a later date!) and it is a wireless card not the conventional magnetic card. Thus a passenger needs not pass through a turnstile. You just walk through the gate. The

card is the ticket but it is also like a data card. This is most important—this card is an information service—it can store data such as the restaurant you have had the meal and the supermarket you buy food from. It also has the same functionality as a credit card. The important point is that this functionality cannot be achieved by a credit company. Japan Railway is a train company and it has a large information infrastructure on its customers. Using this database, they can start new services. The new functionality (unlike a credit card) is the ability to track the consumers' locations by passing through the various tube stations, purchasing habits from one department store to another and transport movements via the train stations as most Japanese people use public transport and not the car. It also has security implications too.

This data in turn drives the activities of Japan Railway services (as opposed to the other way in other systems!) This card has other uses, besides tracking the financial pattern of its clients, and in activating the clients' electrical functions automatically as programmed, on passing through the clients' train stations. All this is done without any buttons—contactless (it is wireless).

This is a new information service and is connected to train operators in the JR Company such as reservation, cashing etc. Thus they can meet demands of their customers—demand lead operations! This IC card was started in October 2001 and its customer base is 6 million. Thus JR Co. has moved from being a train operator to a computer company and from there to an information service company. This is a complete new business. The basic operation as a train operator has not changed and the expansion of core business is achieved due to new technology.

SL25

This detailed account of the application of ADS system on a railway company offers insights into the inter-sectoral dimension from IT software to train operation but also the changes in the practices of the organization impacted by IT to the extent that new jobs and activities are created. This impact is recounted by the Japanese academic:

The new jobs created in JR as a result of this new computer operated technology are jobs, which are driven by customer requirements (demand lead operations). The company now is an IT company—more than credit card with the IC wireless card. Of course the company has its transport infrastructure. New venture is also where new jobs are created. Sometimes it is very risky. Most of the venture companies fail.

Thus a new division has to be created, where the staff communicates with their customers' consumer habitat e.g. restaurants and department stores thus creating new software, new sales persons and marketing people. Also, the running of the trains has to change to meet the demands of the customers and thus the computer system has to change to adapt to this demand (Customer lead demand!). I have been involved in this project. I have students from JR company.

Some of the users of ADS include retail, manufacturing, transportation etc. Some of the new jobs would be to communicate with the restaurants, department stores and other consumer establishment that their train customers use, how to connect with them, how to analyze the data. This may involve new software, new sales people etc. The conventional train operator does not need a lot of marketing people. Now based on customer requirements, they have to know the train sites and their customers' consuming habits in order to cater to their demands. A conventional railway company was about how to start a train and its reliability. Nowadays, the company is dependent on customers and they try to involve in services, which change with customers' changing habits. This is based on centralized system and autonomized system.

Each station has an autonomized computer system (ADS) and if a computer system in another station were to breakdown, it will not affect the operations in the other stations. Also, there must also be a centralized computer operational system to coordinate the overall operation. The new skills for these new jobs besides the new technology (ADS) are new knowledge of ADS by the engineers and programmers.

SL25

Indeed, von Hippel (2006, pp. 101–102) offers examples of closer collaborations in innovative communities in the forms of open source software such as Apache web server software and Fetchmail, an email utility programme and tangible products such as kite surfing equipment. Apache web server software was initially developed by Rob McCool, whilst working at the National Centre for Supercomputing Applications (NCSA) in the early 1990s (von Hippel, 2006, p. 101). He developed Apache, which was used to host webpages and posted on the web for others to use. Webpages are a key element of the Internet infrastructure. This web server software was adopted by a small group of users with extensive user feedback and modifications in the mid-1990s. Towards the end of the decade, it became the most popular web server software used by over 60 per cent of the websites with continuous modifications by users despite strong competition from commercial software developers (von Hippel, 2006, p. 101).

In short, collaborative interactions between users and innovators/producers are a result of readily available knowledge via the Internet supported by advanced technologies such as web server software. These forms of knowledge (from formal qualifications and informal experiences from work and life) supported by available technologies (in this case free of charge) enable creative application of knowledge to produce innovative intangible and tangible goods.

This collaborative approach is at an advanced and enhanced level in the video game area. There appears to be, according to Krotoski (2008) a vibrant independent games culture in Britain where players (both professional developers and enthusiasts) are involved in creating a video game. She cited the example of Spaceship!, which gives developers the opportunity to create a text adventure game in three months. This interactive game without corporate control enables developers to develop their storytelling, design, and programming skills using the Open Source language Inform6. This ability to change the rules of the game such as creation of new characters, fantasy worlds, and weapons is called "modding." Examples of these games include: Quake, Half-Life, and Counterstrike (Sawyer, 2007, p. 205).

Another collaborative trend in video gaming is the need to have human contact as part of gamers' entertainment. The recent commercial successes of Nintendo's Wii, which is outselling the Microsoft's Xbox 360 and Sony's PlayStation 3, suggest that even gamers want casual and social games. The online game, World of Warcraft, has over ten million users alongside others such as Guitar Hero (Schiesel, 2008), Pet Society, and Kidnap! (Franklin and Wray, 2008).

The final observation relates to how closer collaborations between creative knowledge workers, users, and relevant stakeholders can be measured. Interviewees used terms like 'sensitivity to the business context,' 'business intelligence,' and 'soft/human skills.' The interviewees SL28 and SL25 offer some perceptions:

> jobs to do with people and involved in intelligence—business intelligence—where it looks at market trends, competition, product positioning development . . .
>
> Yes, at the end of the day, how successful we are is dependent on how well we have learnt about the external environment which is anything outside ourselves. So we need to put ourselves into the minds of others in order to learn and utilize the experience for the future—that is a soft skill.
>
> Even in the developing countries today, the knowhow is there—relatively speaking and the gap is much narrower like the use of cell phones even in Afghanistan. So it is a matter of time before the whole world is at a level playing field as regards technical skills. So what is left? It must be something to do with the human skills. Increasingly, more cities are going to be global cities with the intermingling of cultures. Thus, human skills which can transcend language barriers, cultural tendencies etc. and the ability to handle these relationships in a globally represented company will be important.
>
> SL28

> I have many engineers to collaborate with many different types of people. These are measurable and are future skills. These are sensitivity skills and they can be measured—when engineers/IT people meet manufacturers, sales people, and customers. Measurement may come in the form of the amount of information the IT/engineer can obtain from the different parties especially we are trying to develop new knowledge.
>
> SL25

The above 'sensitivity' may not be the same as Lash and Urry's (1994) aesthetic sensibilities of beauty and taste but is more related to the previous chapter on advertising, the idea of a being 'social chameleon' or of 'being a general sponge.' These advertising terms refer to the acquisition of socio-cultural knowledge used in a campaign. When applied to IT software, sensitivity may mean being aware both externally and cognitively of current issues/problems/ challenges and being able to think of possible solutions.

Besides the examples of inter-sectoral applications and changes in cultures/ practices in the software community, the above section offers evidence of a closer working relationship between producer and user. This is the 'co-configuration' as studied by Victor and Boynton (1998). Examples include: business clients and software company via the tactical 'mining' of data (SL18); and interactions between producers and users such as Apache web software and Fetchmail (von Hippel, 2006), Quake game (Sawyer, 2007), and World of Warcraft game (Franklin and Wray, 2008).

In addition, this empirical study also identified more nuanced forms of collaborations. They include: relationships with wider range of stakeholders; potential to change the organizational culture and business activities; and measurement of these collaborations. Two interviewees (a professor at an English university (SL19) and a professor at a Japanese university (SL25)) offered evidence of collaboration with a wide range of stakeholders. SL19 suggested that the science community, society at large, and businesses through their use and reliance on software generally and the web in particular interacted in an indirect manner. SL25 specified the direct collaborative nature of his ADS system investigation with multi-disciplinary HEIs, engineers, customers, industry, manufacturers, and Japanese government officials. In terms of changing the activities and cultures of organizations, SL25 related the impact of ADS systems on a train operator. His technology enabled changes in interactions from being a train operator to an IT service company (both as producers) with 6 million users. IT software, viewed as a collaborative tool in the days of accountability and quality control, might also be measured as evidenced by SL25 and SL28. The stakeholders included: software engineers, manufacturers, sales personnel, and customers.

Enculturation Process and Creative Application of Knowledge in the Sector

This part focuses on training, work environment, and education, both formal and informal. These areas are linked to the theoretical framework literature influenced by Csikszentmihalyi (1988), Zuboff (1988), Drucker (1993), Nonaka and Takeuchi (1995) and Reich (2001) in Chapters 3, 4 and culminating in Chapter 6.

The Professor at a university in Tokyo provided the rationale for a more focused trend on research at HEIs:

> Over the last 15–20 years, professors at HEIs did not compete with industry but now, companies are retreating from blue sky research (of 5–10 years

duration) and are more interested in development and commercialization of knowledge into products. Thus the universities are filling this blue sky research gap vacated by companies like Toshiba and Hitachi. The role of HEIs is changing from one as a provider of IT graduates [software] to one of also research of 5–10 years duration. Industries are concerned with 1–3 years' timeframe.

SL26

Creativity for the purposes of this investigation included blue sky research, which involved the acquisition of knowledge required towards the eventual production/and or innovation of new goods, services, or processes.

This emphasis on knowledge acquisition from research was further emphasized by another Japanese professor:

Of course, a university has a mission to teach fundamental technology especially undergraduates and even in graduate school, even in this university we teach very fundamental knowledge and basic technology but now I'm trying, like other leading HEIs, we are trying to add new programmes. Our Economics School has been slow in adapting to new ideas similarly in the Law Schools. Nowadays, in the world, Engineering Schools have to teach advanced technology because it has been rapidly changing and most advanced technology has not been published. Thus my university has tried to establish case study class just one/two years ago for the graduates in the main but also include undergraduates—I asked leading technology companies to participate. I also asked why are they developing new technologies. There are many pathways. Technological developments have many disciplines such as marketing, engineering, commercial (business), intellectual property rights, etc. We (academics) don't have such backgrounds. Without knowledge of such backgrounds, even if we were to develop these technologies, they cannot be utilized, as we do not have the commercial, legal, and other expertise. Even the professors [like SL25] in the technological schools have to know these disciplines/backgrounds."

SL25

The cultures of the above two Japanese universities note a trend towards the acquisition and teaching of cutting edge knowledge and technologies over different disciplines. There are, however, other forms of epistemic cultures in other environments as exemplified by the academic from an English university with his comparison to the Royal College of Art in relation to the types of knowledge and products from these two institutions:

While creativity is important in the development of new technology, if you compare a place like xxx and the Royal College of Art (RCA), a postgraduate place where they think laterally and come up with way out things, you would think how boring this place [xxx] is because people in sciences and engineering have to spend a lot of time assimilating advance knowledge in the areas and without assimilating, they can't graduate and it's a rare individual, but you do find, from technological universities where people such as Bill Gates and the founder of the London International Financial Futures Exchange (LIFFE)—Brian Williamson—one of our former graduates, were exceptions. Who is to say a lot of creativity is needed? You need creativity in research but if you look at somebody like the Tim Berners-Lee, the inventor of the web, he was in effect acting as a software consultant networker trying to make the documentation easier for certain communities. He happened to find a fruitful way of using technology . . .

There are certainly skills there especially research in particular because pushing forward knowledge cannot be done without knowledge where you have a particular training to know what is around in the field before you can sort of say perhaps you do it this way. First thing students learn is that they come up with an idea and its 30 years old. The training in information is the key. Somebody has already developed it and maybe you should industrially develop it. If you were to ask this question, in industry but British industries with some exceptions have not been so wonderful in doing this. If you go to biochemical where knocking at the forefront of the industry within of course a very commercial environment. Perhaps this is one of the reasons why quite a lot of our graduates shy away from standard industry. They are very much in demand if they have the management ability and maybe there is more innovation in smaller companies . . . It's difficult in large companies and the simple reason is that these companies have a lot of investment in existing processes and products and above all, they need to keep financially viable . . . In the IT degree programme, we are not actually concern so much with physics or chemistry. We don't need that but they must have mathematics and people who can solve problems and think abstractly. If they got that ability, then I suppose, for technologists, planning ahead, personal and presentation skills are relevant. You get your mix, and I suspect creativity here does not perhaps depend so much on personal skills or perhaps planning skills but it does involve problem solving and interest in the unknown.

SL21

Bearing in mind that creative application requires knowledge in the first instance, one may ask, how can these be taught? From the micro descriptions of software developing and managing earlier in previous chapter, these creative applications include: solving problems, using anticipatory imagination, realizing power of expression, envisioning, and having ideas. A researcher at a Japanese company provided some insights:

Creativity can be developed. It involves deep and long-time thinking which allows you to make a small difference and accumulated small differences will eventually create innovations.

SL24

This developmental approach to creativity chimed with SL21. Further perspectives on creativity and approaches to teaching abilities such as problem solving required in creative knowledge work are included in the following descriptions by a professor at a university in Singapore:

> Creativity is something which is very difficult to impart. Even when we transfer knowledge: explicit and implicit. Explicit knowledge transfer is very easy in the form of rules, formulae, by example etc. Implicit knowledge is something, which is very difficult to pass onto students. So all we could do is to give them more projects, which are relevant to this industry . . . There are two approaches one can go—as broad as you can or as specialized as you can. xxx is going as broad as possible. Twenty-five per cent of our undergraduate modules must come from outside this faculty e.g. from engineering, business, arts and social science faculties etc. during their undergraduate studies. Most of the common modules in this faculty which we open up to students from other faculties emphasize creative thinking, problem solving etc. Of the six core modules, two are focused heavily on problem solving. We are training our students to be programmers and project managers. Also we have an emphasis on logic before we teach students to do programming. The other twenty-five per cent of the modules offered by our IT faculty related to programme specific e.g. information system, information technology, computer science, computer engineering, e-commerce, and information and communication management. The programmes are very structured: twenty-five per cent on university requirement, twenty-five per cent on faculty requirement, twenty-five per cent on programme and the remaining twenty-five per cent on elective within the faculty. This broad approach hopefully will enable our students to adjust to the outside world and job market.
>
> We also have an industrial advisory committee in order to make our programmes as wide and as relevant as possible. The committee consists of chief information officers from the private sector, and government representatives.
>
> In the past, there were summative examinations and after that continuous assessments and open book examinations pre 2000. Then there were project assessments were introduced. Now each semester has 20 modules, seventy per cent of which have continuous assessments and they account for sixty per cent of the works and others, all continuous assessments. For example, system analysis module is assessed on a project. Continuous assessments could be in the form of assignments, written tests, on the spot test, and peer assessment.
>
> SL31

Technical knowledge and job experience may thus be acquired through a combination of both formal and informal means. In terms of formal education at higher education institutions, interviewees provided examples of activities of inducting their students into professional practices or 'externalizing.' Externalizing refers to non-traditional curricula to include other types of learning such as enrichment modules so that a learner can make the transition between knowledge acquisition and its application in work-related practices easier.

From the interview data, some examples of externalizing activities include: work placements/exchange study programmes, case studies of companies using cutting edge knowledge, enrichment modules providing a holistic learning experience, and diverse assessment approaches to learn soft skills for collaborative working and communication.

The last statement demonstrates the university's vision behind such enculturation practices. A professor from Singapore explained his institution's vision and implementation activities:

> From the xxx perspective, the university has changed . . . from the perspective of a need to be a global competitor as opposed to a national or even a regional competitor. Many of our recent initiatives are designed to meet that challenge e.g. Joint programmes with tier 1 universities from US, Europe and Asia . . .
>
> These take the forms of exchange programmes, joint degree programmes, research projects, and business education with virtual classrooms with Singapore MIT. The other aspect is we have xxx colleges overseas (like Silicon Valley) where we enable our students to spend a year in a specific location where there is a satellite office. The students will be attending a partner university and attached to an organization (private industry). The disciplines the students are involved in covers a wide range e.g. IT. This could also be distance-learning programmes.
>
> . . . Now we design the curriculum in such a way that we have a certain number of enrichment modules as opposed to discipline-specific modules, for example a science graduate may take a language, one of the subjects on the sciences, business school etc. Thus they have to earn a certain number of credits. Students now have to be decision makers and the programmes are modularized. In the engineering programmes, they have one of the highest numbers of contact hours (mid 20s per week and humanities in the high teens) but the impact on the students is tremendous with the follow-up they need to do as homework. We try to reduce the number of formal contact hours and allow more projects and assignments to encourage independent learning rather than rote learning. The result is that the continuous assessment component is rising compared to summative assessment.
>
> . . . Also, we design the curriculum for the students to come up with mini or micro products to earn points. In engineering, a student have to gather sufficient points to graduate by the submission of reports, entering competitions (and points are earned if they win certain ones), assignment based etc. There are also incentives for students to be entrepreneurial, and inventive e.g. getting funding.

SL30

The above enculturation factors affect the way in which workers (collaboratively and individually) apply their knowhow to produce innovative software. The implications for learning and training will be discussed in Chapter 11.

Summary

This Micro dimension section investigated the significance of ICET, studied the working relationships between producers and users, and evidenced the enculturation processes that were required in performing such creative knowledge applications.

The micro-analysis in the IT software sector indicated that there was a degree of commonality in the execution of IT software such as a Simple Mail Transfer Protocol (as described by the Development Manager, SL18) or a game (e.g., World of Warcraft [Franklin and Wray, 2008]) irrespective of where workers were based nationally or internationally. This commonality related to the creative application of: problem solving (researcher at a Japanese company, SL24), having ideas (Deputy Chief Executive of an English computer company, SL17 and Nerland, 2008), applying anticipatory imagination (Managing Director of a Singapore computer company, SL28), using 'power of expression' and 'aesthetic sensibilities' (Professor at a Japanese university, SL27 and Lash and Urry, 1994) and 'sensitivity' (Professor at a Japanese university, SL27; Managing Director of a Singapore computer company, SL28; Professor at a Japanese university, SL25). From the perspectives of inter-sectoral approaches of IT software creation, these included: G2 mobile phone by NTT DoCoMo (Professor at a Japanese university, SL27) and software for the scientific community over different disciplines (Professor at an English university, SL19). An example of the changes in cultural practices included the ADC system when applied to a train operator, which then changed its activities to an IT company (Professor at a Japanese university, SL25).

Creative knowledge activities are influenced by technologies and offer greater scope for workers to be more creative as the automated aspects of their work are taken over by advanced technologies. This creation of higher order level of working is complicated by the proliferation of digital platforms and the need to create supportive software and more emotionally engaging entertainment video games. Advanced technologies offer more space for workers to apply creativity with the added complexity of emotionally connecting with end users through more user-friendly software and interactive (collectively and individually) entertainment formats such as video games.

In terms of the methodological approach of 'co-configuration' (Victor and Boynton, 1998), as identified in the Micro section, closer relationships were found such as the one described by SL18 between its business clients and the company via 'tactical mining of data.' This closer relationship also evidenced that an IT software company could also be an intermediary between the producers/clients and the eventual users, in a way similar to the advertising agencies described in the previous chapter. Other nuanced relationships included: relationships with a wider range of stakeholders (as evidenced by SL19 and SL25; potential to change the organizational culture and business practices and alter the relationships between producer and users (as noted by SL25); and collaboration as a measurement tool (as noted by SL28).

From the methodological approach of 'epistemic culture' in IT software, this section has discussed some commonalities and differences with Knorr Cetina's (2005b) 'epistemic culture' of foreign exchange markets. A commonality is the circulation of knowledge within the IT software community as evidenced in certain creative applications of knowledge such as problem solving and the 'power of expression' described earlier. This is reflected by Grabher's (2004) investigation of the IT software community in Munich, where clients played a significant role towards the execution and manufacturing of software. His study showed that the role is governed by the clients' needs and the nature of the software is for an often-globalized network of users. His typology of network practices: communality (lasting and intense relationships between clients and software organizations); connectivity (transient and weak networks between clients and software companies); and sociality (ephemeral and intense working relationships between clients and computer companies) offers opportunities for engaging with creative knowledge application in this sector.

However, as indicated by the examples of creative knowledge applications of systems developer and systems manager, various applications could be placed on a continuum with 'communality' at one end and 'sociality' at the other. As regards differences to Knorr Cetina's (2005b) 'epistemic culture' (of foreign exchange markets), the IT software sector showed the following trends: wider range of creative knowledge applications relating to 'power of expression' and 'sensitivity,' creation of new jobs via the development of advanced technologies, greater emphasis on creativity with the support of software to facilitate the automation of lower level work such as data organization, and greater relevance to everyday activities whether they relate to work (e.g., Word and Excel software) or leisure (online games).

Macro perspective of the information technology software sector

This section is based on the microsociology methodological approach by Knorr Cetina and Bruegger (2002a, p. 909) as discussed in Appendix 1 on methodology. The previous sections discussed the IT software knowledge workers in three types of work (intra-sectoral, inter-sectoral, and changes to practices). This was based on the empirical data of interviewees from England, Japan, and Singapore and showed that a global network of work existed. These approaches have implications beyond the immediate context of the software companies toward a global dimension, explained here. This section provides evidence of an established presence in the ICT and the IT software sector in the global context.

Information and Communications Technology (ICT) Industry in the Global Context

The revenues of the largest 250 ICT firms in 2011 amounted to US$ 4,602.6B.[1] These were classified into eight sectors of the industry in order of revenue size: telecommunications (the largest), electronics and components, IT equipment, IT services, communications equipment, semiconductors, software, and Internet (the smallest). The software sector accounted for three per cent of the total revenues. Based on the same data, the research and development (R&D) spend to revenue per sector for 2011 showed that the software sector was the highest with 13.8 per cent.[2] The ICT industry is highly significant in terms of global reach; even though the software sector accounted for only three per cent of the industry revenue, the sector had the highest percentage in terms of the R&D spend to revenue.

From the perspective of the largest technology companies in 2012 as ranked by revenue,[3] Apple Incorporated was the largest with US$ 156.5B (Appendix 4, Table 4.1). Three observations are noted. The first relates to the revenue size. Each of the five largest companies had revenues over US$ 100.0B, which is bigger than the GNI of Morocco with US$ 97.6B (ranked 59th in 2011).[4] The second relates to the location of the companies. Of the 12 largest IT companies, six are based in US, four in Japan, and one each in South Korea and Taiwan. The presence of IT companies from South Korea and Taiwan indicated the increasing significance of the IT sector in those countries relative to the traditional countries of US and Japan. The third observation relates to the industry type. Of the largest 12 technology companies, only one was a software company, Microsoft, ranked eighth with revenues of US$ 73.7B and market capitalization (i.e., number of shares multiplied by the market price per share) of US$ 225.0B. It represented the third largest market capitalization of the 50 firms. The reason for this might be due to a high price placed on its shares relating to high market expectations of this IT company headed by Bill Gates. Even though this software sector of the IT industry was the second smallest in revenue (of the top 250 IT firms in 2011), the significance of its share market price should not be lost. It could relate to the market expectation of the software company coming up with innovative products and services, which in turn drives the IT market. If true, then the creative applications of knowledge in the software sector will be a crucial element in creating innovative goods.

IT Software Sector in the Global Context

The investigation in this part is on IT software, which according to Hoch et al. (1999, p. 7) "largely drives and enables today's economy" and the following argument is developed here: 1) the important scaffolding of the knowledge economy is the information, communications, and electronic technologies (ICET); 2) the IT software sector forms a significant part of this industry where innovative goods may be created; and 3) in order that innovative goods are created, there needs to be creative approaches to applying knowledge.

The world packaged software market in 1999 was US$ 154.9B (OECD, 2002) and in 2001, US$ 196.2B, an increase of 27 per cent over this three-year period. In 2001, the US accounted for 49 per cent and the OECD countries, which included the US, accounted for 95 per cent of the world packaged software market. The world of packaged software was dominated by the US and OECD nations. In the context of the total ICT market in 2001, the packaged software market amounted to 9 per cent (OECD, 2002).

Even though this investigation does not involve cross-country comparisons, it may be useful to relate the size of the world packaged software market in 2001 (base on OECD figures) to a country with a similar size Gross National Income[5] (GNI) to get a sense of the significance of this market. The two countries with the nearest GNIs in 2002 (the nearest available data) were Sweden (with GNI US$ 231.8B), and Austria (with GNI US$ 192.1B), which were ranked nineteenth and twentieth largest in the world,[6] respectively. Countries with smaller GNIs included Saudi Arabia, Poland, and Norway. Allowing for the discrepancy in comparative years and the relatively small size of the software market in relation to the IT market, the countries with equivalent GNIs are found in the second tier of the top ten countries with the largest economies.

In 2011, Software Magazine carried out a survey of the largest 100 software companies. The total revenues for 2010 came to US$ 235.0B.[7] Table 4.2 in Appendix 4 showed the largest 20 software companies. This survey gave a more up to date indication of the size of the software market compared to the OECD data. It focused on the software revenues of the 100 largest software companies, which included the sale of licenses, maintenance, subscription, and support and excluded revenues from custom software development. Thus, the Software Magazine methodology is different from the OECD methodology and comparison is not possible.

However, from the Software Magazine survey, four observations might be ascertained. The first relates to the dominance of Microsoft, the largest of the software companies with revenues of US$ 54.27B in 2010, accounting for 23.1 per cent of the total revenue of the largest 100 software companies. Relating to the first observation is the significance of the four largest companies in revenue terms which accounted for 46.7 per cent of the total revenue of the largest 100 software companies.

The third observation is the dominance of the US companies (12 out of the 20 largest software companies), Japanese (with three) and European countries such as France (with two), Finland (with one), Germany (with one) and Sweden (with one). If all 100 companies were included, the country with the most was US (with 63), followed by Japan (with 10), France (with three), the UK (with four) and Germany (with three). Organizations in England and Japan were featured in this investigation alongside those from a small but developed nation, Singapore.

The final observation relates to the maturity of the software sector. It is no longer a cyclical sector but reliant on steady income streams of subscriptions, support, and maintenance activities. The 2008 financial crisis did not affect the revenues from the sector with only single digit decline.[8] Moschella emphasized the maturity of the sector by suggesting that IT firms were becoming service providers and also IT customers. Instead of customers just buying computer systems to make their business more effective, they were using IT to create services for their clients thus becoming part of the sector's supply chain (Moschella, 2003). He also cited examples like Amazon, E*Trade, eBay, and Microsoft, and traditional companies like banks, insurance companies, and publishers who were becoming part of this sector's supply chain. For example, one of the software vendors, Sun, is becoming more of a software firm than a manufacturer of power plants for computing utilities (Economist, 2003).

In summary, the software sector is a significant part of the IT industry where innovative products and services are created and ICET is an important structure of the knowledge economy.

Summary

This Macro section provided a global context in terms of the ICT and the software markets. ICET is an important structure of the knowledge economy. The significance of the software sector is undisputable and creative applications of knowledge are required to innovate new products and services in the global marketplace. The global presence of IT software companies appeared to be more homogeneous (compared to the localized networks of the ad agencies) from the perspective of more global acceptance of software products such as Microsoft Word and World of Warcraft. However, local clients as evidenced by SL18 drove the needs and nature of the required software product, which required the 'tactical mining of data.' From the inter-sectoral approaches, local contexts dictated the nature of the creative knowledge application in the case of the Japanese train operator (SL25). However, also notable is the wider global application of the G2 mobile phone by NTT DoCoMo in Japan (as evidenced by SL27). In short, there is a mixed picture of localized and globalized dimensions at play in the IT software sector.

Observations and insights

This chapter on IT software in the Micro dimensions and Macro sections identified three creative knowledge approaches: intra-sectoral, inter-sectoral, and the changes in cultures/practices together with the related abilities and skills. The chapter provided nuanced and modified versions of co-configuration and epistemic cultures, which were used as methodological approaches to studying the empirical data.

Notes

1. OECD (2012) Internet Economy Outlook 2012 DOI: 10.1787/9789264086463-en. Top 250 ICT firms by sector, 2000 and 2011: USD millions in current prices and number of employees. [Online]. Available at: http://www.keepeek.com/Digital-Asset-Management/oecd/science-and-technology/oecd-Internet-economy-outlook-2012/top-250-ict-firms-by-sector-2000-and-2011_9789264086463-table15-en. [Last accessed 31st December 2012].

2. Although this research does not involve cross-country comparison, it may be useful to relate the sector's expenditure to a country with a similar size Gross National Income (GNI). The country with the nearest GNI in 2011 was Germany (US$3,617.7B), which was ranked fourth largest in the world. Countries with smaller GNIs in 2011 included France, UK, and Italy. Based on data from the World Bank. [Online]. Available at: http://databank.worldbank.org/databank/download/GNI.pdf. [Last assessed 30th December 2012].

3. 'Top 50 Global Technology Companies'. [Online]. Available at: http://www.computer wire.com/companies/lists/list/?listid=7A7B551F-A6C8–47AC-B3AE-3879873B5E23. [Last accessed 31st December 2012].

4. Although this study does not involve cross-country comparison, it may be useful to relate the sector's expenditure to a country with a similar size Gross National Income (GNI). Based on data from the World Bank. [Online]. Available at: http://databank.worldbank.org/databank/download/GNI.pdf. [Last assessed 30th December 2012].

5. World Bank. [Online] Available at: http://web.worldbank.org. [Last accessed 10th December 2008].

    GNI includes all production in a domestic economy of a country (i.e., Gross Domestic Product) and the net flows of factor income—e.g., rents, profits, and labour income from abroad. These are based on the World Bank's official estimates of the size of economies in current US dollars using the Atlas method. The Atlas method smooths exchange rate fluctuations by using a three-year moving average, price-adjusted conversion factor.

6. World Bank (2006) 'World Development Indicators, Size of the economy, providing gross national income figures for 2004.' [Online]. Available at: http://web.worldbank.org. [Last accessed 10th December 2008].

7. 'Global Software Top 100—Edition 2011. [Online]. Available at: http://www.software top100.org/global-software-top-100-edition-2011. [Last accessed 31st December 2012].

8. 'Global Software Top 100 Edition 2011: The Highlights. [Online]. Available at: http://www.softwaretop100.org/global-software-top-100-edition-2011-*the-highlights.* [Last accessed 31st December 2012].

10 Forward

Introduction

In order to study the creative application of knowledge in the knowledge economy, this investigation used a combined interdisciplinary and relational approach (Guile, 2010) in the literature review drawing on the disciplines of economics, management, psychology, and sociology. It found an eclectic and discipline-centric view of creative application of knowledge where knowledge work was regarded as generic with definite roles and functions allocated to specific jobs. This study argued for a more nuanced understanding of creative knowledge work and identified three approaches: intra- and inter-sectoral roles and functions of specific jobs, and the influence of these workers on operational cultures and practices.

In order to support the three creative knowledge work approaches, empirical data from two sectors and three countries was used. The two chosen sectors were advertising and IT software. The former was associated with a 'conventional notion of creativity' where work could be related to the arts and humanities and the latter to information technologies. A common feature was aesthetic sensibilities. Three developed countries of England, Japan, and Singapore were chosen to investigate non-generic creative knowledge work on a global scale.

Two methodological approaches: a two-way relationship between producers and users—'co-configuration'—and a use of technology to circulate knowledge—'epistemic cultures'—were chosen to investigate the empirical data and provide a more contextualized understanding of the three approaches of creative knowledge working. The final methodological approach of 'microsociology' was used to investigate creative application of knowledge by individual workers from a globally networked perspective.

This final chapter summarises the investigation. Chapter 1 provided a topic of study: *"creative knowledge work in the knowledge economy"* with a discussion of knowledge and knowledge work, the research questions, and lines of argument.

Having established the basis for the investigation and its structure, Chapter 2 reviewed the contemporary discourse on knowledge and the 'new economy.' Scholars and experts reviewed were drawn from the disciplines of economics, management, and sociology. The literature review showed that: a) there were differing perspectives on the knowledge economy, b) it had no clearly defined boundaries, and c) it was in transition. This research also provided evidence of linkages between the industrial and the knowledge-based economies and the term 'connective dimensions' was conjugated to emphasize these links. The connective dimensions were: a) an increasing digitalization of knowledge goods alongside tangible goods, b) an increasing global network of businesses, and the influence of culture on knowledge workers (beyond the scope of this study), and c) closer collaboration between the producers and users/consumers of knowledge economy goods.

In Chapter 3, the context of work in the knowledge economy was examined. Definitions of knowledge and knowledge work were defined and it was concluded that knowledge was derived from an individual vision and could also be collaborative. Human inspiration and creativity were the main driving force in the production of these new forms of goods and services. Three themes were identified: i) individuals who applied cognitive skills, abilities, and creative personalities to create new goods, ii) workers who used their education, formal and informal training, previous work experiences, and tacit skills as well as abstracted data to improve their work processes, and iii) workers who collaborated by pooling their individual knowledge in the organizations where they worked.

In Chapter 4, four descriptions of creativity in relation to knowledge work were identified and investigated. Social-cultural dimensions, which involved interacting with people in the work environment in varying degrees, were featured in all four approaches with varying emphasis on individual or collaborative styles of working. Two themes were highlighted: a) people and their skills, abilities, and attributes involved in creative knowledge work, and b) the types and degrees of enculturation.

Chapter 5 presented the conceptual framework of creative knowledge work through a two-dimensional matrix. This framework was drawn from the two connections between the identified themes from the Chapter 3 on knowledge work and Chapter 4 on creativity. The connections are: a) the supportive environments that facilitated the enculturation of the workers into established and/or new routines and workplace practices, and b) individuals who applied their cognitive skills, abilities, and personalities in their work activities either individually or collaboratively. The two dimensions were: individual and collaborative styles of working, and single and multi-contexts. Each of the quadrants incorporated the four work approaches (Chapter 3) together with the four creativity descriptions (Chapter 4).

The next four empirical chapters discussed the advertising and IT software sectors wherein the descriptions of the three approaches (intra- and inter-sectoral and influences of workers on the cultures and practices) of creative applications of knowledge were examined alongside micro dimensions. This included the significance of ICET, closer working between producers and users, enculturation practices, and macro descriptions of the sectors.

This final chapter—Chapter 10—is structured as follows: following the introduction, the second section considers the contributions of this study in response to the five research questions posed in Chapter 1. The third section focuses on the implications of the findings from the perspectives of education and work practices. It concludes with recommendations.

Contributions to Creative Knowledge Work

The findings from the analyzed empirical data offer a complex picture of creative knowledge work in the knowledge economy where workers use a combination of creativity, abilities, talents, skills, and knowledge towards the eventual production of products and services.

This investigation identified a definition of creative knowledge work, which included a complex combination of skill sets or 'creative knowledge work (ckw) capacities.' In addition to this definition, the study also noted three types of creative knowledge work and the necessary work conditions for it to occur.

Creative knowledge workers use a combination of creative applications to perform their functions/roles in the knowledge economy including: anticipatory imagination, problem solving, problem seeking, and generating ideas and aesthetic sensibilities. These creative approaches were identified in four roles: copywriting, creative directing, software programming, and systems programme managing in two sectors: advertising and IT software. The manner in which each of the creative applications is applied is dependent on the role(s) of the creative workers.

Taking aesthetic sensibility as an example, for a creative director, it is a visual imagery whether still or moving via a camera lens and for a software programmer, it is the innovative technical expertise in which the software is written.

There are also creative applications which are specific to the two sectors. These include an emotional connection in the advertising sector, and the power of expression and sensitivity in the IT software sector. Terms such as 'general sponge,' 'social chameleon,' and 'in tune with the zeitgeist' were identified which the creative knowledge workers used to identify emotionally with their potential audience in ad making. From the IT software perspective, creative knowledge workers used 'sensitivity' creative application to ascertain business intelligence and as a measurement of information the software worker might obtain from various parties.

Along with the creative applications, a creative knowledge worker requires abilities and aptitudes to carry out her/his role. Passion for one's job was generic to the roles investigated in the two sectors and for copywriters, this passion was identified with fun, enjoyment, and happiness in carrying out the role alongside attributes such as honesty (regarding the product), confidence, and patience in finding the appropriate copy. As with the other roles, a creative worker in software programming requires team working and interpersonal skills in order to communicate effectively with those from other disciplinary backgrounds and training. As regards the managerial roles of creative directing and systems programme managing, the abilities to create a vision for the job in hand, to convince, strategize, execute, and plan towards the eventual completion of the given task (such as a campaign or a software) are necessary capacities. Linking these abilities and capacities are collaborative ways of working, which the findings from this study have identified. The two modes of working ranged from individual to collaborative where a worker might be doing either or both depending on the specific activity. The ability to traverse between these two work modes alongside the relevant creative application are part of the complexity of this style of working.

Aside from these creative processes, abilities, and skills, which are significant to knowledge work, in addition, workers require an understanding of various forms of knowledge. These are related to disciplines such as those from the humanities (e.g., literature), and the creative arts such as painting and music (e.g., popular and classical varieties). Creative knowledge workers also require technical-related knowledge such as mathematics and computer sciences (e.g., software engineering) and physical sciences (e.g., physics) though there are distinctions in the two sectors. In the IT software sector, technical knowledge of software languages is especially significant for programmers as ascertained in the findings. However, the degree of technical expertise may be less for a programme manager, as only knowledge of the relevant software language is necessary to understand the issues for communicating with the team of developers and testers. The technical knowhow for a creative director relates only to the understanding of the possibilities of technologies (such as graphics and typography) in order to capitalize on the technical wizardry. The technical specialists are then required to execute the creative director's vision.

The above types of disciplinary knowledge may appear in explicit formats, which can be learnt from formal programmes at teaching institutions such as higher education and professional institutions alongside other skills and abilities relating to presentation, communication, and team working. As ascertained in the findings, there was other non-disciplinary knowledge, which was not explicit but tacit in nature. Interviewees mentioned tacit experiences from their past work and life experiences, which they used to draw upon in performing their creative knowledge work. This form of knowledge was harnessed collectively as a team (of an advertising campaign or a software programme). This collaborative approach to working, especially with roles such as creative directing and software programme managing, requires tacit knowledge of the strengths and weaknesses and the needs and wants of the related team members (knowledge of psychology). This form of working may occur within the organization, as a stand-alone group for a specific project in the organization, or as a sub-contracted team outside the organization. Within this role, creative knowledge workers may perform their activities individually and/or collectively as part of their contribution to the project. The findings also brought out some characteristics of collaborative working such as the varieties of stakeholders such as sub-contracted groups, and the indirect relationships between clients, workers (of an ad agency), and consumers.

In addition to the definition of ckw capacities of a creative knowledge worker, the findings also identified three levels of creative knowledge applications and how they related to intra-sectoral approaches, inter-sectoral approaches, and changes in culture/practices in the sectors (Appendix 2).

Finally, complex creative knowledge work needs a supportive environment. One such environment relates to the supporting technical base. Based on the findings, ICET is viewed as an organizational tool, a source of ideas (such as the Internet), and a way of modelling a concept. It may also be applied to inter-sectoral activities such as software for cross-disciplinary applications. This organizational tool enables creative knowledge workers to devote their energies to multi-faceted activities such as analysis of huge data sets and the enabling of new jobs such as webpage designing. ICET enables workers to spend more time on advanced activities, which leads to the intensification of creative applications.

Lastly, it was noted from the findings that a supportive environment focussed on training, work environment, and education. These will be discussed in relation to the implications of the above findings in the next section.

Implications

The previous section highlighted the contributions of this study and provided a platform for this section to investigate the implications of the findings and their contributions from the perspectives of: prior to work and at work settings.

The definition of ckw capacities in the previous section offered an illustration of how creative knowledge workers used their knowledge, abilities, skills, and creativity towards the eventual production of goods and services in the knowledge economy. The acquisition of these capacities occurred over time either informally and/or formally. This approach to ckw capacities acquisition and application relates to the notion of lifelong learning, which will be used as a starting point to understanding creative knowledge workers' learning.

The definition of lifelong learning by the Organization for Economic Co-operation and Development (OECD), offers a conceptual framework to discussing the implications of this research:

> Lifelong learning offers an appropriate framework for addressing these issues. The new idea underpinning 'lifelong learning for all' goes beyond providing a second or third chance for adults and proposes that everyone should be able, motivated and actively encouraged to learn throughout life. This view of learning embraces individual and social development of all kinds and in all settings—formally in schools, vocational, tertiary and adult education institutions and non-formally at home, at work and in the community. The approach is system-wide; it focuses on the standards of knowledge and skills needed by all regardless of age.
>
> (OECD, 1996, p. 15)

This conceptualization by policy makers of learning in settings such as educational institutions, workplaces, home, and community reinforces the findings of this investigation as explained earlier. Additionally, lifelong learning may also be viewed as a precursor to creative knowledge working in the knowledge economy. The OECD policy refers to some dimensions of the knowledge economy in terms of "information technologies, globalization, trade liberalization, changing nature of work, and use of knowledge and skills" (OECD, 1996, p. 15).

However, the definition did not mention in any specific detail how different forms of learning such as formal and informal learning might occur in relation to specific work contexts. Nor did it offer any insights into the potential learning and working that occurred in collaborative ways. It also did not encapsulate the wider definition of creative knowledge work capacities such as creativity and forms of creative knowledge applications, or people's abilities and talents. Nevertheless, this definition offers space for discussion on a) creative knowledge work from the perspective of acquiring such knowledge, skills, and abilities at an early stage prior to becoming creative knowledge workers and b) the implications for creative knowledge workers.

In addition to the OECD definition of lifelong learning, the policy of the European Communities, entitled: 'The European Interest: Succeeding in the age of globalization' (Commission of the European Communities, 2007) is relevant here. The goal of this paper was to ensure the 'making of the EU into a dynamic, competitive, knowledge based society'. EU policy makers noted:

> Both globalization and technological change risk increased inequality, opening up the gap between the skilled and the unskilled. The best solution is to help each individual to adapt, by improving the quality and availability of education and training for all ages.
>
> (Commission of the European Communities, 2007, p. 8)

The strategy highlighted:

> There is a growing interest in "flexicurity." This can help people to manage employment transitions more successfully in times of accelerating economic change. By upgrading their skills, and protecting people rather than particular jobs, it helps people to move into better paid, more satisfying jobs, or even start their own businesses.
>
> (Commission of the European Communities, 2007, p. 8)

It can be seen that policy makers are interested in understanding how individuals can become more successful economically. Indeed, in relation to this, the findings from this research makes an invaluable contribution because it illustrates and explains how individuals work and learn through various professional and personal activities, which are inter-related and mediated (OECD, 1996; European Union (EU) Commission, 2000).

This investigation also noted that workers worked collaboratively around common commercial goals within or outside of their professional organizations and this has implications for transnational policy because it indicates the importance to policy makers of understanding, harnessing, and facilitating the supporting environment and activities, which enables workers to carry out their creative knowledge work effectively.

This penultimate section is divided into two sections: a) on educational/ academic perspectives (prior to getting into work) and b) on work/practice perspectives (performing roles/functions at work), as a device to investigate learning and working, which are inter-connected activities for creative knowledge workers.

Educational/Academic Perspectives of Creative Knowledge Work

The OECD's (1996) definition of lifelong learning which suggests second and third chances for adults to learn throughout their lives is a significant recognition as it suggests that adults engaged in routes to becoming creative knowledge workers are not necessarily clear at the outset how their careers will map out. In addition, as delineated in the findings, having a knowledge base of more than one discipline requires effort and time.

From the formal educational perspectives, the findings showed that aspiring creative knowledge workers needed to access and acquire disciplinary knowledge in the technical areas, alongside mathematics, computer sciences, physical sciences, and psychology, depending on their roles and functions of creative work. They also needed to have knowledge of the humanities and creative arts and the emphasis of these forms of disciplinary knowledge is dependent on the nature of the work in the sector, as identified in the data analysis. The implications for the programme offered at teaching institutions such as the higher education and professional-related institutions are relevant here.

The diverse programmes offered at universities give aspiring creative knowledge workers access to disciplinary knowledge of the humanities and the creative arts. Based on empirical data, when they are enrolled on a computer science programme at teaching institutions such as HEIs, candidates are offered multi-disciplinary modules. This approach has implications for the course structure, teaching resources, and administration. Courses require opportunities for the candidates to take part in modules (e.g., psychology and the creative arts) other than those related to the programmes which they have enrolled on such as computer sciences. The acquisition of non-course related disciplinary knowledge provides them with opportunities to acquire multi-disciplinary knowledge. Lecturers should also be aware of learners from differing disciplines and training backgrounds and reflect on the choice of relevant and identifiable teaching resources and how these may impact the candidates' learning. Related to this, is the assessment issue where due to differing training, a computer science learner may not be as confident or accomplished as a humanities student in writing an essay. This may have implications in the provision of writing assistance by the institution. The administration and organization of inter-related programmes require careful discussion and planning with the related programme coordinators and management to provide a user-friendly structure for learners' accessing interdisciplinary provisions. The above approaches may create issues for smaller teaching institutions when they are focused on the humanities or the sciences and technical areas. This issue may be circumvented by collaborations with nearby institutions (and/or using other modes of learning such as digital-related programme offers).

The above suggestions have implications for policy makers (within and beyond the HEIs) and resource allocation/funding. In the era of budgetary tightening since the global recession which started in 2007/8, the sciences, technologies, engineering, and medicine progammes have been promoted as more relevant to the labour market (Commission of the European Communities, 2007) of the knowledge economy. As this study evidenced, 'softer areas' of the creative arts and the humanities are just as significant in creative knowledge working and this has significant implications for policy making and resource allocation especially in the current global economy when austerity is still being contested.

Related to the identified ckw capacities are creative applications such as problem solving, problem seeking, generation of ideas and sensitivities, abilities, and aptitudes such as confidence, strategizing, and execution of a task, and collaborative working, formal learning opportunities which offer aspiring creative knowledge workers opportunities to fine tune their skills and knowledge.

From the empirical findings, these opportunities include: master classes with practicing professionals to present 'real-life' innovative cases (and advertising briefs) for students, inclusion of professionals on advisory panels to provide insights and inputs into course specifications, use of a wide variety of assessment approaches such as group activities, projects, peer and continuous assessments to encourage collaborative working, problem solving and seeking, presentation skills, and to encourage and foster confidence building.

The term 'externalizing' was used in the earlier chapters to refer to non-traditional curricula, which supported aspiring creative knowledge workers to make the transition between knowledge acquisition and its application. The empirical findings showed that teaching institutions have an important role to play in facilitating this significant transition. These may include: exchange programmes, joint degree programmes, research projects, business education with virtual classrooms in HEIs and organizations, internships, work placements, competitions (external of HEIs), and acquisition of funding for projects.

The above discussion also has relevance to aspiring workers before the higher education stage when they need to access and acquire a broad education of several disciplines. This approach to ckw capacities acquisition resonated with the Creative Director of an advertising agency in London (SL2) when she commented, it was necessary "to be a general sponge" and to acquire "knowledge and things that inspire from films and people you hear and things that you see and places that you visit." These capacities take time to access and acquire and a higher education qualification offers a short window of opportunity to becoming a creative knowledge worker, depending on the roles/functions and the sector.

The time for accessing and acquiring a creative knowledge capacity base also has implications before the higher education stage and this relates to the compulsory education stage. A broad education of the sciences, humanities, and creative arts would offer the most relevant platform to becoming a creative knowledge worker. This approach to a broad education has implications on the variety of subjects up to the higher education level and includes the necessity for a learner to have a minimum core subjects such as: sciences, humanities, languages, creative arts, and access to differing cultures and perspectives, all of which are critical in a globalized world of work.

As with higher education, the offer of a broad curriculum in the compulsory years has implications for policy-making and funding where providing equitable educational opportunities are prerequisites to having a creative knowledge workforce which is determined by having the creative knowledge work capacities and not monetary privileges.

In the case of informal learning, for some learners in creative knowledge work, this is another platform to acquire skills and training. This informal learning, which can include team and individual sport activities (and foster team spirit and competitiveness), can occur at a) home with supportive parents, families and friends, b) learning institutions before the higher education stage, or c) HEIs and/or professional institutions.

This type of tacit learning is relevant to creative knowledge work as evidenced from the findings and may include sources such as films, museums, theatres, music, art festivals (e.g., literature, poetry, and art), outdoor pursuits, cultural sites, and sports fixtures. The relevant emotional connections with the audience may be in advertising or video gaming. Creative knowledge workers need to be able to draw on their knowledge base to create emotional connections, which are humorous, literary, artistic, or based on life experiences. The ability to access these activities, from both sciences and humanities allows workers to design creative applications with broad appeal. That is why a wide knowledge base is critical. This informal learning has implications for policy makers and resource allocation because it indicates that society needs a vibrant and diverse cultural environment. Using England as an example, the Department for Culture, Media and Sport (DCMS) (2001) highlighted the cultural and financial significance and contributions to society. At the present time, under austerity measures, the funding to these creative industries has been decreased and this budgetary tightening has implications for creative knowledge work. This is because if access to a vibrant and diverse cultural landscape is lessened, it ultimately affects the eventual production of innovative products and services.

As indicated in the findings, the creative applications of aesthetic sensibilities are required in both sectors of advertising and video gaming. The potential impact of funding cuts to these sectors is real and policy makers and funders should be made aware of the implications of this to the economy. A vibrant and diverse cultural environment is necessary for stable economic growth and a vibrant civil and cultural society. Total reliance on the sciences and technologies is risky as indicated by as the findings here.

Furthermore, as the knowledge economy relies on an ICET infrastructure, having sufficiently robust, efficient, and accessible advanced technologies are important for creative knowledge activities. Equitable access to such advanced technologies by all age groups irrespective of financial means supports and encourages potential and aspiring creative knowledge work. From education perspectives, we turn now to the work perspectives of creative knowledge.

Work/Practice Perspectives of Creative Knowledge

In the previous section, the importance of transitional support from learning to working settings was discussed, as evidenced by the finding of this study. This approach ties-in with the work environment where creative knowledge workers apply theoretical and tacit knowhow which is acquired in educational settings.

While this delineated pathway may be truer for one role (e.g., software developing) rather than both (e.g., creative directing), it depends primarily on the sector and the role as well as the contexts, and these will indicate which learning, formal and/or informal, are necessary to acquire skills and capacity for creative knowledge work.

Being engaged in full-time work does not necessarily imply that learning ends, because learning from work practices continues. These are different and specific and depend on the roles, organizations, jobs, environment, and activities of the worker. For instance, having a supportive work environment, as illustrated by the empirical findings, such as a mentoring system for novice workers, can offer a smoother transition from learning to a work environment. This learning process has implications for business organizations.

From the perspective of creative knowledge workers, organizations can contribute to a collaborative type of learning by offering conditions which facilitate creativity and support towards the acquisition of relevant ckw capacities and their application. This form of learning from work-based practices involves both disciplinary and tacit knowledge (e.g., work and life experiences) and can be acquired either collaboratively and/or individually depending on the nature of the activity. This approach to learning in work has implications for businesses in providing supportive conditions for creative knowledge workers and supporting their lifelong learning whilst at work

This approach, as evidenced in the empirical findings, may include in-house training by expert colleagues or external specialists from the relevant field. These organizations can encourage their creative workers to acquire knowledge in different disciplines through enrolment at formal learning centres (e.g., university programmes) or engagement in informal settings (e.g., cultural events) and these activities may be within or outside of work. Additionally, these organizations may support external training at professional bodies such as the British Computer Society, the American Society for Quality and the International Software Testing Qualification Board, which offer certification in IT software courses. Businesses such as Microsoft also offer short courses and training in various modes of learning, e.g., face-to-face and online. In short, the organization has a critical role to play in facilitating a lifelong learning workforce in various learning and working modes.

At an informal level, outsourced creative knowledge workers may be offered opportunities to engage in continuous professional development. This approach may include provision of financial assistance and space for these workers. The opportunities can be related to their creative knowledge work. One support feature is DukeDollars, which is an online community that answers technical questions. This learning and working approach offers workers opportunities to establish and build networks for future creative projects.

As evidenced in the four empirical chapters, certain creative knowledge workers such as software developers may need or want to acquire on going skills and capacities such as a software language or knowhow of a new media platform. In the case of advertising, creative directors working in the pharmaceutical industry may want to have a greater understanding of innovative technological platforms for product/brand campaigns. These working and learning approaches enable the workers to acquire additional capacities as well as providing them with different approaches to utilizing their newly acquired capacities, both explicit and tacit. These offer opportunities of expanding not only their disciplinary knowledge but also their tacit knowledge in relation to work practices. This expanded capacity base acts as a resource in the application of creative knowledge such as problem solving, generation of ideas, and anticipatory imagination.

The drawing on the tacit experiences of work practices and life experiences is an important element of creative knowledge working. From an intra-sectoral working perspective, the Managing Director of a Singaporean company (SL28) urged creative workers to "put ourselves into the minds of others in order to learn and utilize the experience for the future—that is a soft skill." This form of tacit knowledge related to creative knowledge workers' life experiences and noted how they should be able to emotionally connect with their consumers. This meant that they ought to be able to reflect on the social, cultural, and political world around them and use this to create an innovative good/product/service, to which consumers could relate. Interviewee SL28 managed a software computer business which had operations throughout South East Asia, and he referred to how software developers' soft skills enabled him to produce software applications relevant to the organization's customers.

Another creative knowledge work example was described by the Professor at a Japanese university (SL25) which shows a change in cultures/practices and the complex and tacit relationships between disciplinary knowledge and its application for the benefit of mankind. He explained this in relation to the

ADS system operated by the Tokyo train operator: "If we create new knowledge [explicit] based on the leading countries and companies to the needs of the people (nationally and globally) that is pure knowledge." He stressed that this explicit knowhow was needed for the benefit of mankind and its utilization required creative applications such as problem seeking and solving and anticipatory imagination to convert the knowhow to products and/or services. In this example, the creative applications involved a more efficient supply of trains to cater to increased customers' (6 million) needs, and the provision of added functionalities such as on demand switching on the customers' homes' heating and lighting facilities on activating the train IC wireless cards at their home station turnstiles ahead of their journeys. This link between explicit knowhow and enabling a better quality of life requires tacit knowhow and the imagination to be able to anticipate the needs of customers or anticipatory imagination.

Organizations need to acknowledge these complex ways of creative knowledge working, which draw on formal and informal learning and explicit and tacit forms of knowhow. The implication for these organizations relates to the provision of supportive working environments for workers. As illustrated above, when complex roles are required, a collaborative-individual approach to working is optimum. Using the ADS as an example, it was shown how creative knowledge workers needed to operate in teams to create a large enough resource so that they could pool together their disciplinary knowledge. This indicates that team spirit and team working abilities are required.

Other resource sources of a more explicit nature are libraries (e.g., public, professional, and HEIs) and digital sources (e.g., Internet). The DukeDollars as a digital resource offers both explicit (in the form of texts) and tacit where IT professionals draw on their past work and life experiences to offer possible solutions to specific issues. The access to these resources (both human and non-human), as illustrated by the empirical findings, facilitates workers in complex activities. There are implications for businesses, organizations, policy makers, and entrepreneurial enterprises in facilitating workers with access to a robust and vibrant infrastructure, supportive business networks, and collaborations with relevant institutions and organizations.

A creative knowledge worker may have different roles/activities depending on the teams, disciplinary knowledge, training, and perspectives. Negotiating these requires some of the ckw capacities identified in the previous section. Discussions, idea generation, convincing others about an idea, and leadership qualities are some of the critical and necessary abilities and attributes. These creative work capacities were discussed in the previous section. The complexity of creative knowledge work, whether it be an in-house team or a sub-contracted team, is dependent on the differing disciplinary knowhow, professional perspectives, and the team members' experiences (tacit and explicit). All these have important implications for business organizations. How the organization supports the complex roles that creative workers undertake will impact the potential completion of the innovative product/service.

One of the complexities of creative knowledge working is the ability to have the confidence to fail and try again. Interviewees such as the President and Creative Director of an agency in Singapore (SL12) noted that in addition to confidence and patience there must also be the ability to take risks and the "willingness to try and not afraid to fail" and to try again. These attributes are relevant because the trial and attempt each time pushes the boundaries of knowledge and creativity further towards the fashioning of innovative products and services. Indeed failures along the way are almost de rigueur and provide invaluable experiences to a worker individually or the team as a collective. The recognition of these experiential approaches to creative working is significant in promoting experimentation. If this work approach is acknowledged as a positive, then there are implications for business organizations because generally speaking, failures are anathema because of the financial implications. This tension between facilitating experimentation on the one hand and the pressure to achieve maximum profitability for the shareholders and directors of the business entities on the other has consequences.

In addition to working in business organizations, as with some of the interviewees who participated in this study, entrepreneurial activities also have a degree of uncertainty with financial and creative rewards or 'flexicurity' (Commission of the European Communities, 2007, p. 8). Fostering these activities alongside the possibilities of unemployment and financial collapse has implications for policy makers. Transnational communities and global business networks need to confront this style of working where part-time employment is a possibility and where there is the necessity for the creation of supportive networks with financial and/or re-training opportunities so that creative knowledge workers can to be supported during uncertain periods of their working lives.

The previous section discussed the contributions of this study, which included: a) a nuanced definition of creative knowledge work, b) capacities for creative knowledge work, c) creative knowledge workers' applications, abilities, and attributes, d) the need for multi-disciplinary knowledge, work, and real-life experiences (including explicit and tacit forms), e) three levels of working, and f) the requisite supportive environment for this work.

The implications of the contributions are investigated in this section from the perspectives of a) prior to work and b) at work. These have repercussions for learning, both formal and informal, and are dependent on the different types of learning institutions which workers have access to throughout their professional lives whether they are working in business organizations or as entrepreneurs. These were discussed from the workers', organizations', and policy makers' perspectives in terms of accessing, acquiring, and applying the workers' skills and capacities towards the eventual production of innovative products and services. This included a discussion of the complexities of different styles of working.

The two sections indicated that traditional notions of learning and working as distinct activities required re-assessing as this study showed that learning and working were closely related for creative knowledge workers. Policy makers at institutional (e.g., HEIs, schools, and sectors), network (e.g., European Community and OECD) and country level (e.g., England, Japan, and Singapore) need to re-conceptualize how learning and working activities may be carried out by workers either collaboratively or individually. From the findings as discussed in this chapter and in the four empirical chapters, HEIs academics have already emphasized the inter-relationships of learning and working on their programmes and externalizing offers. For the future more integrated approaches to learning and working should be encouraged at all levels.

Way Forward

To sum up, this investigation has offered new understandings in terms of the interdisciplinary and relational nature of creative knowledge work in the knowledge economy. It provided a distinctive conceptual framework, drawing upon economics, management studies, psychology, and sociology.

Three specific approaches to creative knowledge work were identified: intra-sectoral, inter-sectoral, and influences on operational cultures/practices.

The study defined creative knowledge work capacities from the perspectives of creative knowledge applications and the necessary abilities, skills, and talents.

Recommended further areas for research might include: cross-country comparisons to examine the impact of culture on creative knowledge working, an examination of more creative sectors to get a richer understanding, and the inclusion of users/consumers' perceptions to provide a fuller more holistic scope. This would help provide a more comprehensive picture of this new style of working in the knowledge economy, which is currently missing in the literature.

The global recession, which began towards the end of 2007, has had a huge impact on the knowledge economy and knowledge working. In advertising, there is evidence of a reduction in advertising revenue to traditional media such as television but an increase in online advertising. The UK was the first major economy to register a larger Internet advertising spend than television in the first half of 2009 (Sweney, 2009) and this digital trend is set to continue. In IT software, video gaming remains largely unaffected perhaps due to the fact that gamers stay at home with their games rather than go out.

The knowledge economy is firmly established, though it will always be in transition and the digitalization of products will grow at a faster rate relative to equivalent tangible products due to cost and delivery advantages. In the current uncertain economic climate with austerity measures and budget cuts, nurturing creative knowledge workers is crucial and vital for sustainable economic growth and a healthy cultural and civil society. Human ingenuity in its complex and nuanced creative knowledge application forms a vital part of the knowledge economy and it must be acknowledged, understood, and nurtured.

11 Coda

To date, this book has investigated the nuanced and complex creative application of knowledge of the knowledge workers in the digital/knowledge economy. The study started with an eclectic and discipline-centric perspective of knowledge work where it was regarded as generic with definite roles and functions for specific jobs. However, this investigation has identified three specific approaches for creative knowledge work and the enculturation factors that are needed to support this type of work. The specificities of this type of work in the knowledge economy are *highly contextualized* as clearly delineated in both the empirical chapters (Chapters 6—9) of the two sectors of advertising and IT software, and the theoretical framework drawing from the literature reviews of four disciplines from economics, management, sociology, and psychology.

It is with the above caveats in mind that this Coda chapter offers readers, who may not have the inclination or the time to carefully read through the previous ten chapters, a basic understanding of this distinct investigation of creative knowledge work in notation format. It starts off with a reminder of the salient points of the theoretical framework and is followed by the eclectic definition of knowledge for the purposes of creative working in advertising and IT software and finishes with a generic definition for this type of work in the knowledge economy. This generic approach may perhaps facilitate users of this book and provide such as practitioners and academics in the areas of the knowledge economy, managers of work organizations and teaching institutions, policy makers, education researchers, and socio-development change agents a quick overview of this study. From the definition of knowledge, three micro perspectives of creative work are indicated. The next three listings consist of the creative applications, the creative abilities and attitudes, and the supportive enculturation factors for creative work. In each of these listings, it provides specificities for the advertising and IT software sectors and generic approaches for the knowledge economy.

1. Components of the conceptual framework of creative knowledge work:

    *   Two dimensions—Styles of Working (Individually and Collaboratively) and Contexts (Single and Multi-).

- The quadrants consist of the themes from the literature reviews of knowledge work and critical perspectives of creativity and knowledge work.
- Each quadrant consists of amplifications of work approaches (e.g., 'Geeks & Shrinks' (Reich, 2001), 'Engineers & Officers' (Nonaka and Takeuchi, 1995), 'Informated workers' (Zuboff, 1988), 'Specialists & Operators' (Nonaka and Takeuchi, 1995) and 'Technologists' (Drucker, 1999)) and creative descriptions by Csikszentmihalyi (1988), Gardner (1999), Sternberg et al. (2004), and von Hippel (2006).

2. Definition of creative knowledge for the:

- Advertising sector—Disciplinary knowledge (e.g., literature, films, and current affairs which are usually explicit/codified forms); knowledge of past work and life experiences (usually tacit forms); knowledge of team members and technical knowledge (e.g., of graphics, typography, and digital media).
- IT software sector—technical knowledge (e.g., software languages of Java and C+++); knowledge of other disciplines (e.g., physics); knowledge of popular culture; knowledge of team members and knowledge of past work and life experiences.
- Generic level of the knowledge economy—disciplinary knowledge (e.g., humanities, creative arts, and technical-related subjects of mathematics and computer sciences and physical sciences) and non-disciplinary knowledge (e.g., tacit experiences from past work and life experiences from individuals and/or groups).

3. Three micro approaches of creative knowledge work:

- Intra-sectoral (e.g., "The aura a brand gives off is emotional" and "Power of expression").
- Inter-sectoral (e.g., ". . . the buzz word is integrated . . ." and "Autonomized computer system (ADS) system in the Tokyo train operator").
- Changes in cultures (e.g., "total communication approach" and "collaboration with HEIs and industry").

4. Creative applications of knowledge work consist of a complex combination of skill sets or 'creative knowledge work (ckw) capacities' for the:

- Advertising sector—aesthetic sensibilities; anticipatory imagination; emotional connection; and problem seeking and solving.
- IT software sector—aesthetic sensibilities; anticipatory imagination; "power of expression"; problem seeking and solving; and "sensitivity."
- Generic level of the knowledge economy—aesthetic sensibilities; anticipatory imagination; and problem seeking and solving.

5. Abilities and aptitudes of creative knowledge workers for the:

    •   Advertising sector—ability to capitalize on the technical wizardry; "ability to have fun, enjoyment and happiness"; confidence; collaborative style of working; empathy with the audience; honesty about the product; leadership abilities (e.g., persuasion and visualization); interpersonal and intrapersonal abilities; patience; presentation skills; and vision.

    •   IT software sector—collaborative style of working; generation of ideas; ability for hard work, focus and concentration; interpersonal and intrapersonal abilities; leadership abilities (e.g., implementation, motivation, and persuasion); passion for the job; and vision.

    •   Generic level of the knowledge economy—collaborative (and individual) styles of working; confidence; fun, enjoyment, happiness and passion for the job; honesty (regarding the product); generation of ideas; interpersonal and intrapersonal abilities; and patience. For leadership roles, they require vision for the job; and the abilities to convince, motivate, strategize, execute, and plan towards the eventual completion of the given task.

6. Facilitative enculturation factors for supporting creative knowledge work at the:

    •   Advertising sector—accessing of popular cultural activities including art, drama, sports; advisory panels; information, communications and electronic technologies (ICET) (in addition to the technical aspects, there are ways of engaging with the audience using media platforms, differing screen sizes, multi-tasking facilities, temporal dimension, and heightened exposure to advertising); on-the-job training (formal and informal); mentoring structure and supportive people such as parents and friends.

    •   IT software sector—ICET infrastructure such as the Internet and software; formal and informal learning environments such as higher education institutions and accreditation bodies offering externalizing/ enrichment curricula (formal) and DukeDollars and YouTube (informal); and work placements/exchange study programmes.

    •   Generic level of the knowledge economy—accessing of popular cultural activities; ICET (as organizational and accessing tools, a source of ideas, and a way of modelling a concept); on-the-job training; formal and informal learning environments; mentoring structure; and supportive people.

Appendices

Appendix 1
Methodology

This appendix focuses on the methodology and is structured as follows: the first part provides a justification of the methodological approach, the second part focuses on interviews, and the third part is on data analysis.

The methodological approach in this research reflects Walford's (1987, p. 5) notions of research as "a profound pragmatic and down-to-earth activity" and researchers who "grapple with the innumerable problems that confront them in their task." These issues occurred in the various stages of the investigation from the review of literature sources, set up of interviews, the capture of the interview data, to the analysis of the empirical data in relating to the theoretical framework. In order to relate the research questions, theoretical framework, and empirical data, this investigation subscribes to Smyth and Shacklock's (1998, p. 5) notion that research is an ongoing activity where "experiential and inter-pretive faculties" may continue even after the empirical data has been captured. With these notions in mind, the methodological approach takes its stance in this research from the fifth line of argument as indicated in the first chapter where a creative worker may be involved in a closer collaboration with the end user and that this closer relationship between producer and user is a new dimension in the knowledge economy. In order to adhere to this approach, this investigation used Victor and Boynton's (1998) idea of 'co-configuration' where:

> . . . work occurs at the interface of the firm, the customer, and the products or services. It requires constant interaction among the firm, the customer, and the product. The result is that the product continuously adjusts to what the customer wants. Co-configuration creates customer–intelligence value in products or services, where the lines between product and customer knowledge become blurred and interwoven.
>
> (Victor and Boynton, 1998, p. 14)

This two-way relationship was utilized as a guide in the data analysis to the extent that interviewees acknowledged that creative knowledge work involved actively seeking feedback from users or customers. In this manner, identifica-tion of versions of co-configuration in the data was possible. These nuanced versions included closer and wider collaboration between creative directors in the advertising agencies, clients, and potential users through the use of focus groups, collaborations of campaign-making between agencies and their clients with different products/services, and varied working relationships between IT workers, higher education institutions, customers, manufacturers, and government officials. As a result of this methodological approach, a separate section 'Closer working between producers and users in the sector' was included. In addition, other relevant examples of collaborative forms of creative knowledge working are discussed in the four empirical chapters (Chapters 6 to 9).

Another aspect of this methodological approach relates to the literature review in Chapter 2. Literature from Bell (1973) on 'theoretical knowledge' was reviewed and knowledge, as applied in the culture industries as argued by Lash and Urry (1994), was included. Lash and Urry's advocacy of 'cultural industries' knowledge was seen to be relevant in the knowledge application in the knowledge economy, as was additional literature by the sociologist, Lury (2004), on knowledge applications in the advertising industry. Also incorporated was Knorr Cetina's (2005a) argument in favour of 'epistemic cultures,' which facilitated the use of technology to circulate knowledge. This approach, like 'co-configuration,' was used as a guide to interrogate the data. From the 'epistemic cultures' perspective, examples were sought of how interviewees applied knowledge through their use of technology in their creative knowledge working. These nuanced versions of working in the epistemic cultures of advertising or IT software included: the shaping of the products/services derived from different institutions such as a higher education institution in London and the Royal College of Art in London, the application of technology for the benefit of mankind, and the notion of the 'golden thread' in an advertising campaign such as Orange. It was thought that by using epistemic cultures of working as a methodological approach, new insights into creative knowledge work could be studied. This form of analysis also pointed the way as to how certain ways of creative working could impact on the work culture, which is one of the three types of creative knowledge work to be investigated. Further descriptions of this style of work are discussed in the four empirical chapters (Chapters 6 to 9).

The third and final aspect of the methodological approach refers to the use of case study to study this phenomenon of creative knowledge work. The use of case study is explained by writers, such as Denscombe (1998), Cohen, Manion and Morrison (2000) and Robson (2002), as a legitimate methodological approach as it provides a deeply contextual analysis of a complex issue. This methodological approach has been used in the social sciences and its advantages are that it has a 'strategy' to study a 'specific contemporary phenomenon' in a 'real-life context,' and it involves 'research' using analysis and evaluation, which is 'empirical' in methodological approach using 'multiple methods of evidence' (Robson, 2002, p. 179).

Case study, according to Yin (cited in Robson, 2002) is defined as follows:

> Case study is a strategy for doing research which involves an empirical investigation of a particular contemporary phenomenon within its real life context using multiple sources of evidence.
>
> (Yin, cited in Robson, 2002, p. 178)

The case study methodological approach was thought to be the most appropriate and relevant in the context of this investigation because first of all, the 'strategy' taken was one of a long-term approach using the two methodological approaches of 'co-configuration' and 'epistemic cultures.' With regard to 'research,' it was taken here to be an investigation, including analysis and evaluation into creative work in the knowledge economy with particular focus on the two sectors of advertising and IT software. The 'empirical investigation of a particular contemporary phenomenon' referred to a specific case of creative application of knowledge in three countries and two sectors of the knowledge economy. The rationale for choosing the three developed countries of England, Japan, and Singapore was to investigate the hypothesis that in the knowledge economy, businesses were globally networked and not 'nationally bound' (Knorr Cetina and Bruegger, 2002a, p. 909), and thus the commercial activities within national boundaries would be less significant in comparison to industry/sector global activities (Castells, 2000; Reich, 2001; Knorr Cetina and Bruegger, 2002a). The three countries were used as guides to study non-generic approaches of creative knowledge work on a global scale as mentioned in lines of argument number nine in Chapter 1.

The literature reviewed three themes: knowledge and the knowledge economy, knowledge work, and creativity and knowledge work in Chapters 2 to 4, and was based on generic descriptions of this type of work. This investigation sought to examine a more contextualized understanding of creative knowledge working. By choosing a methodology which involved three developed countries, this investigation used the data captured from the interviews from professionals and academics to study the descriptions of creative knowledge work from the perspectives of different roles in a sector (i.e., intra-sectoral work), similar roles in different sectors (i.e., inter-sectoral work), and the influence of creative knowledge workers on the culture in which they operate. From the perspectives of intra-sectoral work, they included the different roles of copywriters and creative directors and the use of focus groups in the advertising sector, and the roles of IT software developers and IT programme managers in the IT software sector. In terms of the intra-sectoral work, some of the patterns included the advertising of different products from dissimilar clients to create new product brands and markets, the use of IT software to generate competitive advantage and use of outsourcing activities over diverse sectors and disciplines and the development and application of IT software, i.e., 'modding' or changing the rules of video games. In terms of the influence of creative knowledge workers on the culture they operated in, the patterns included the ethical approaches to advertising, the 'three-dimensional trust,' and 'golden thread' approaches to ad making, the concept of 'power of expression' in IT software activities, and the mining of customers' data using IT software to create added advantage for clients.

This particular methodological approach of investigating the specific workings of this type of knowledge workers from a global perspective was influenced by the concept of 'microsociology' expounded by Knorr Cetina and

Bruegger (2002a) who used it to study global financial markets. They viewed microsociology as "the installation of global social forms that are not nationally bound . . . and are . . . largely dependent on individuals and social microstructures" (Knorr Cetina and Bruegger, 2002a, p. 909). They suggested that this phenomenon "allows a thick description of the specificities of global social forms that could complement network approaches" (Knorr Cetina and Bruegger, 2002a, p. 910).

The focus on professionals and academics to study the three types of creative knowledge work (i.e., intra-sectoral, inter-sectoral, and influences on the work cultures) enabled this study to identify two sectors: advertising and IT software. As indicated in Chapter 1, the advertising sector was chosen following a literature review of creativity where artistic endeavours epitomized this form of activity (MacKinnon, 1962; Barron, 1983). This business sector might also be associated with a 'conventional notion of creativity,' where the work related to the arts and humanities appeared to be advertising (Quah, 1999; Howkins, 2001; Reich, 2001). IT software was chosen for this study because it was found to be a sector which was closely related to one of the major characteristics of the knowledge economy, i.e., information technologies (Quah, 1999; Castells, 2000; Reich, 2001). These two sectors along with others in the knowledge economy are globally networked businesses and justify the approach taken here, that of a global network investigation to creative knowledge working.

Thus 'an empirical investigation of a particular contemporary phenomenon' for this study involves the study of creative knowledge working over three countries and two sectors. By focussing on the thick description of this style of knowledge work, it became possible to show the common practices of specific roles such as copywriting, creative directing, IT software developing, and IT software programme managing from the two sectors and across the three countries that creative knowledge work may not necessary be 'nationally bound' but exists as 'global social forms' to an extent. This 'micro' approach to investigating creative knowledge work was used as a guide to make a case for the existence of two sectors in a 'macro' context where organizations such as advertising agencies have networks of global offices. From the perspective of this study, using the principle of 'microsociology' or the 'micro' dimension of rich descriptions of creative knowledge workings of a sector, complements the 'macro' dimension of that sector. The micro and macro descriptions of the two sectors are featured in the four empirical chapters.

The 'real-life context' might be referred to a new area such as the knowledge economy where creative productions of knowledge goods were carried out where 'multiple methods of evidence' might include not just empirical evidence from interviews but also from the literature review. The rationale for choosing the professionals and related academics in the two sectors and from the three countries will be discussed in the next section supporting Appendix 2. This appendix provides salient details of the 31 interviewees in the three countries and the two sectors together with indications of intra-sectoral and inter-sectoral workings, influences on the work cultures, gender, role, organization, and country.

The second part of this appendix on methodology focuses on interviews. The research questions relating to the data for collection included: 1) the understanding of the knowledge economy, 2) the characteristics of the workers working in this context, 3) the manner in which creative application of knowledge is understood by key actors in the two sectors, 4) the importance of creativity in this type of work and 5) the necessary contexts for creative knowledge work. The interviews were carried out with experts in their fields to obtain their perceptions and opinions of creative application of knowledge towards the production of knowledge goods within and between sectors and the impact of it on workers' cultures.[1] Details of the interviews included: 16 in the advertising sector and 15 in the IT sector, and of the total of 31 interviews, 18 were professionals in the two sectors and 13 were academics in higher education institutions. The justification of carrying out the interviews by country was on the basis of their physical location. The use of academics in related fields was justified on three grounds namely; 1) a balanced view of the public and private sectors, 2) for triangulation purposes, and 3) academic perspectives. The data triangulation relied on data from both sectors of advertising and IT software, two types of interviewees, practitioners, and academics as well as in-depth literature review of both sectors. The interviewees were selected on the basis of their seniority and prominence in their field of expertise. Those who had an established name in their field would be recognizable by accolades (for those in industry), awards, or prizes in the advertising sector or by the quality of journals where research was published (for the academics).

The selected interviewees were contacted by a Letter of Introduction and a follow-up email. Each interview was carried out in English and recorded using a micro cassette recorder, if possible, and if not, then notes were made during the interview. In all cases, a post-interview written summary of salient points was made. A transcription was done at a later stage in order to formalize the interview in codified form. Two topic guides (a list of questions relating to the research questions as referred to in Chapter 1) were drawn up for the two types of interview questioning (for professionals and academics) so that the interview process was purposive, responsive, interactive, and systematic. The topic guides were designed to field open-ended and sensitive probing questions, and as a result, a systematic and comprehensive approach was achieved, which catered to both groups. It consisted of the use of flexible and interactive interviews, identification of key topics and issues, formulation of questions in the interview, follow-up on relevant issues, and the use of probes and prompts.

This investigation uses data and theory triangulation approaches (Patton, 1980; Denzin, 1989). Data triangulation is relevant as the study relies on data from two sectors (advertising and IT software), two types of interviewees of practitioners and academics, and literature sources relation to the two sectors. Theoretical triangulation links concepts from various disciplines to the conceptual framework. Denzin's (1989) rationale of the theoretical triangulation is explained as:

> The necessity of considering theoretical triangulation as an integral figure of the research process is shown in those areas characterized by a high degree of theoretical incoherence . . .
>
> (Denzin, 1989, p. 240)

The third and final part of the appendix on methodology relates to the data analysis. The analysis of the data from the fieldwork occurred in several stages. A post-interview write-up noted the interviewer's perceptions in order to act as a reference/refresher at a later stage. This interviewer's impression was transcribed. The tapes of each interview were listened to several times at later stages in order to re-familiarize the points that came up in the interviews. Notes were made from the selected representations of points, themes, and/ or quotations resulting from repeatedly listening to the tapes. The tapes were transcribed from the selected representations of themes and quotations for the purposes of the study and in relation to the research questions. After transcription of the recorded interviews, the tapes were re-listened to in order to pick out any possible themes that might have been missed.

Cohen et al. (2000, p. 282) suggested four stages in data analysis. These included: generating units of meaning; classifying, typologizing and ordering the units of meaning; using narratives for richer descriptions; and interpreting the data. These were useful in the data analysis of the transcribed interviews. 'Generating units of meaning' (Cohen et al., 2000, p. 283), with the issues of ascertaining more than one possible topic in a sentence or paragraph aside, was a credible first step to breaking the text into bite-size chunks of different meanings. This consisted of a listing of units after listening to the tapes and referring to the notes and transcribed interviews. The 'use of narratives' (Cohen et al., 2000, p. 282) was particularly helpful in providing colour and insights to the four empirical sector chapters (Chapters 6 to 9) such as the relationships between the advertisers (e.g., copywriters and creative directors) and their clients and users. In this situation, passages of the interview text would be used in the relevant context. The 'interpretation of the data' (Cohen et al., 2000, p. 282) involved relating the analysis to the theoretical framework, as was discussed in Chapter 5 and went beyond the generic outlines of the theoretical framework. It created newer and richer analysis in terms of creative knowledge working within (intrasectoral) and between sectors (inter-sectoral) and the impact this work had on operational cultures. An example of this related to the creative skills and talents, which were specific to the creative knowledge jobs such as creative director in advertising and to a sector such as IT software.

Turning to 'classifying, typologizing, and ordering units of meaning' (which related to Robson's (2002) second-level coding exercise), Miles and Huberman's (cited in Cohen et al., 2000, p. 283) strategies, both referred to by Cohen et al. (2000) and Robson (2002), should be mentioned as they were useful in this aspect of the data analysis. This approach of data analysis occurred after the 'first-level' coding of listing words, ideas, and themes from the transcribed interviews such as creative skills, abilities, and personalities. The relevant strategies included: noting patterns, themes, and trends; counting frequencies of occurrence of words, ideas, and themes; clustering of items into categories, types, and classifications; using metaphors to connect data with theory; subsuming particulars—i.e., linking specific data to concepts; factoring—i.e., bringing a large number of variables under a smaller number of conceptual variables; making contrasts and comparisons; and making conceptual coherence between the theoretical framework and the data.

Appendix 2

Details of Interviewees

Table A2.1 Details of interviewees

Interviewee	Role	Country	Sector	Intra-sectoral	Inter-sectoral	Influence on work cultures	Gender	Organization
SL1	Creative Director	E	A	✓		✓	M	Advertising agency
SL2	Creative Director	E	A	✓	✓	✓	F	Advertising agency
SL3	Creative Director	E	A	✓			M	Advertising agency
SL4	Academic	E	A	✓	✓	✓	F	Higher education institution
SL5	Professor	E	A	✓			M	Higher education institution
SL6	Copywriter	J	A	✓		✓	M	Advertising agency
SL7	Art Director	J	A	✓	✓	✓	M	Advertising agency
SL8	Creative Director	J	A	✓			M	Advertising agency
SL9	Art Director	J	A	✓		✓	M	Advertising agency
SL10	Creative Director	J	A	✓			M	Advertising agency
SL11	Professor	J	A	✓			M	Higher education institution
SL12	President/Creative Dir.	S	A	✓	✓	✓	M	Advertising agency
SL13	Copywriter	S	A	✓		✓	M	Advertising agency
SL14	Founder	S	A	✓			M	Advertising agency
SL15	Professor	S	A	✓	✓	✓	F	Higher education institution
SL16	Professor	S	A	✓	✓	✓	M	Higher education institution

(Continued)

Table A2.1 (Continued)

Interviewee	Role	Country	Sector	Intra-sectoral	Inter-sectoral	Influence on work cultures	Gender	Organization
SL17	Co-founder	E	I	✓	✓	✓	M	IT company
SL18	Development Manager	E	I	✓		✓	M	IT company
SL19	Professor	E	I	✓		✓	M	Higher education institution
SL20	Professor	E	I	✓		✓	M	Higher education institution
SL21	Academic	E	I	✓	✓	✓	M	Higher education institution
SL22	Director	J	I	✓			M	Research institution
SL23	Senior Manager	J	I	✓			M	IT company
SL24	Researcher	J	I	✓			M	IT company
SL25	Professor	J	I	✓	✓	✓	M	Higher education institution
SL26	Professor	J	I	✓		✓	M	Higher education institution
SL27	Professor	J	I	✓	✓	✓	M	Higher education institution
SL28	Managing Director	S	I	✓	✓	✓	M	IT company
SL29	Chief Executive Officer	S	I	✓			M	IT company
SL30	Professor	S	I	✓		✓	M	Higher education institution
SL31	Professor	S	I	✓		✓	M	Higher education institution

Key:

SL1 Interviewee J Japan
F Female S Singapore
M Male A Advertising
E England I IT software

Appendix 3

Macro Perspectives of the Advertising Sector

Table A3.1 Top 25 advertising organizations in 2008[2] and 2001[3]

Rank 2008 (2001)	Advertising Organization	Revenue US $ millions 2008 (2001)
1 (3)	Omnicom Group[4]	12,694 (7,404)
2 (1)	WPP Group[5]	12,383 (8,165)
3 (2)	Interpublic Group of Companies[6]	6,554 (7,981)
4 (4)	Publicis Group	6,384 (4,769)
5 (5)	Dentsu[7]	2,930 (2,795)
6 (-)	Aegis Group	2,200 (-)
7 (6)	Havas	2,094 (2,733)
8 (9)	Hakuhodo DY Holdings[8]	1,392 (874)
9 (-)	MDC Partners[9]	547 (-)
10 (-)	Alliance Data System	487 (-)
11 (10)	Asatsu-DK	454 (395)
12 (-)	Media Consulta	415 (-)
13 (12)	Carlson Marketing Group	413 (356)
14 (-)	Microsoft Corp. (Avenue A/Razorfish)[10]	368 (-)
15 (-)	Photon Group[11]	314 (-)
16 (19)	Cheil Worldwide[12]	300 (142)
17 (-)	IBM Corp. (IBM Interactive)[13]	278 (-)
18 (-)	George P. Johnson Cos.	253 (-)
19 (-)	Sapient Corp. (Sapient Interactive)[14]	241 (-)
20 (-)	STW Group	235 (-)
21 (-)	Grupo ABC de Communicacao (ABC Group)	228 (-)
22 (-)	Clemenger Group[15]	220 (-)
23 (24)	Cossette Communication Group	218 (95)
24 (-)	LBi International[16]	211 (-)
25 (-)	Media Square[17]	206 (-)

Table A3.2 Top 100 world's most valuable brands 2012[18] and 2003[19]

Rank 2012 (2003)	Brand	US $ million 2012 (2003)	Country of origin
1 (1)	Coca-Cola	77,839 (70,453)	USA
2 (50)	Apple	76,568 (5,554)	USA
3 (3)	IBM	75,532 (51,767)	USA
4 (-)	Google	69,726 (-)	USA
5 (2)	Microsoft	57,853 (65,174)	USA
6 (4)	GE	43,682 (42,430)	USA
7 (8)	McDonald's	40,062 (24,699)	USA
8 (5)	Intel	39,385 (31,112)	USA
9 (25)	Samsung	32,893 (10,846)	South Korea
10 (11)	Toyota	30,280 (20,784)	Japan
11 (10)	Mercedes-Benz	30,097 (21,371)	Germany
12 (19)	BMW	29,052 (15,106)	Germany
13 (7)	Disney	27,438 (28,036)	USA
14 (17)	Cisco	27,197 (15,789)	USA
15 (12)	Hewlett-Pickard (HP)	26,087 (19,860)	USA
16 (16)	Gillette	24,898 (15,978)	USA
17 (45)	Louis Vuitton	23,577 (6,708)	France
18 (24)	Oracle	22,126 (11,263)	USA
19 (6)	Nokia	21,009 (29,440)	Finland
20 (74)	Amazon	18,625 (3,403)	USA
21 (18)	Honda	17,280 (15,625)	Japan
22 (23)	Pepsi	16,594 (11,777)	USA
23 (-)	H&M	16,571 (-)	Sweden
24 (15)	American Express	15,702 (16,833)	USA
25 (35)	SAP	15,641 (7,714)	Germany
26 (33)	Nike	15,126 (8,167)	USA
27 (-)	UPS	13,088 (-)	USA
28 (43)	IKEA	12,808 (6,918)	Sweden
29 (38)	Kellogg's	12,068 (7,438)	USA
30 (39)	Canon	12,029 (7,192)	Japan
31 (22)	Budweiser	11,872 (11,894)	USA
32 (31)	JP Morgan	11,471 (10,897)	USA
33 (37)	HSBC	11,378 (9,642)	Britain
34 (-)	Pampers	11,296 (-)	USA
35 (21)	Nescafe	11,089 (12,336)	Switzerland
36 (-)	eBay	10,947 (-)	USA
37 (-)	Zara	9,488 (-)	Spain
38 (-)	Gucci	9,446 (-)	Italy
39 (42)	VW	9,252 (6,938)	Germany
40 (20)	Sony	9,111 (13,153)	Japan
41 (59)	Philips	9,066 (4,464)	Netherlands
42 (47)	L'Oreal	8,821 (5,600)	France
43 (52)	Accenture	8,745 (5,301)	Bermuda
44 (76)	Thomson Reuters	8,444 (3,300)	Canada
45 (14)	Ford	7,958 (17,066)	USA
46 (40)	Heinz	7,722 (7,092)	USA
47 (56)	Colgate	7,643 (4,686)	USA
48 (41)	Goldman Sachs	7,599 (7,039)	USA
49 (29)	Dell	7,591 (10,367)	USA

(Continued)

Rank 2012 (2003)	Brand	US $ million 2012 (2003)	Country of origin
50 (13)	Citi (Citibank)	7,570 (18,571)	USA
51 (-)	Siemens	7,534 (-)	Germany
52 (62)	Danone	7,498 (4,237)	France
53 (-)	Hyundai	7,473 (-)	South Korea
54 (26)	Morgan Stanley	7,218 (10,691)	USA
55 (-)	Audi	7,196 (-)	Germany
56 (32)	Nintendo	7,082 (8,190)	Japan
57 (60)	Nestle	6,916 (4,460)	Switzerland
58 (-)	AXA	6,748 (-)	France
59 (48)	Xerox	6,714 (5,578)	USA
60 (67)	Adidas	6,699 (3,679)	Germany
61 (75)	Caterpillar	6,306 (3,363)	USA
62 (-)	Allianz	6,184 (-)	Germany
63 (73)	Hermes	6,182 (3,416)	France
64 (49)	KFC	5,994 (5,576)	USA
65 (79)	Panasonic	5,765 (3,257)	Japan
66 (-)	Sprite	5,709 (-)	USA
67 (46)	MTV	5,648 (6,278)	USA
68 (-)	Cartier	5,495 (-)	France
69 (-)	Facebook	5,421 (-)	USA
70 (70)	Tiffany & Co	5,159 (3,540)	USA
71 (57)	Avon	5,151 (4,631)	USA
72 (-)	Porsche	5,149 (-)	Germany
73 (89)	Nissan	4,969 (2.495)	Japan
74 (-)	Visa	4,944 (-)	USA
75 (83)	Shell	4,788 (2,983)	Britain/Netherland
76 (-)	Santander	4,771 (-)	Spain
77 (-)	3M	4,656 (-)	USA
78 (-)	Adobe	4,557 (-)	USA
79 (86)	Johnson & Johnson	4,378 (2,706)	USA
80 (54)	Kleenex	4,360 (5,057)	USA
81 (-)	Jack Daniel's	4,352 (-)	USA
82 (-)	Burberry	4,342 (-)	Britain
83 (-)	Johnny Walker	4,301 (-)	USA
84 (87)	Prada	4,271 (2,353)	Italy
85 (-)	John Deere	4,221 (-)	USA
86 (51)	Pizza Hut	4,193 (5,312)	USA
87 (-)	Kia	4,089 (-)	South Korea
88 (93)	Starbucks	4,062 (2,136)	USA
89 (-)	Corona Extra	4,061 (-)	Mexico
90 (85)	Smirnoff	4,050 (2,806)	Britain
91 (-)	Ralph Lauren	4,038 (-)	USA
92 (-)	Heineken	3,939 (-)	Netherlands
93 (-)	Blackberry	3,922 (-)	Germany
94 (-)	Mastercard	3,896 (-)	USA
95 (-)	Credit Suisse	3,866 (-)	Switzerland
96 (44)	Harley-Davidson	3,857 (6,775)	USA
97 (65)	Yahoo!	3,851 (3,895)	USA
98 (88)	Moet & Chandon	3,824 (2,524)	France
99 (-)	Ferrari	3,770 (-)	Italy
100 (36)	Gap	3,731 (7,688)	USA

Appendix 4

Macro Perspectives of the Information Technology Software Sector

Table A4.1 Largest 12 technology companies in 2012 (in US$B)[20]

Rank	Company	Country	Industry	Revenue US$B.	Market Cap. US$B.
1	Apple Inc.	USA	Hardware/Electronics	156.5	573.5
2	Samsung Electronics	South Korea	Semiconductor/ Electronics	149.0	162.0
3	Hewlett-Packard	USA	Hardware	120.4	23.0
4	Foxconn	Taiwan	Electronics	117.5	27.2
5	IBM	USA	Hardware/Software	106.9	225.2
6	Panasonic	Japan	Electronics	99.7	22.7
7	Toshiba	Japan	Electronics	74.4	19.3
8	Microsoft	USA	Software	73.7	225.0
9	Sony	Japan	Electronics	67.4	22.1
10	Dell	USA	Hardware	62.1	16.2
11	Fujitsu	Japan	Hardware/Software	54.5	7.7
12	Intel	USA	Semiconductor	54.0	98.2

Table A4.2 Largest 20 software companies (in US$ millions)[21]

Rank	Company	Revenue 2011	Country
1	Microsoft	54, 270	USA
2	IBM	22, 485	USA
3	Oracle	20, 958	USA
4	SAP	12, 558	Germany
5	Ericsson	7, 274	Sweden
6	HP	6, 669	USA
7	Symantec	5, 636	USA
8	Nintendo	5, 456	Japan
9	Activision Blizzard	4, 447	USA
10	EMC	4, 356	USA
11	Nokia Siemens Network	4, 229	Finland
12	CA	4, 136	USA
13	Electronic Arts	3, 413	USA
14	Adobe	3, 177	USA
15	Alcatel-Lucent	2, 561	France
16	Cisco	2, 383	USA
17	Sony	2, 083	Japan
18	Hitachi	1, 939	Japan
19	Dassault	1, 885	France
20	BMC	1, 843	USA

Notes

1. This activity occurred from November 2001 to April 2002.
2. Advertising Age. [Online]. Available at: http://adage.com/agencyfamilytrees08/. [Last accessed 7th October 2008].
3. Advertising Age. (2002), 22 April 2002, p. 30. These advertising organizations include advertising agencies, public relations companies, sales promotion, direct marketing, and other non-advertising, i.e., marketing-related activities.
4. Includes DDB, BBDO and TBWA, to name a few of the advertising agencies.
5. Includes Grey Global Group, formerly ranked 7 in 2001 and Cordiant Communications Group, formerly ranked 8 in 2001.
6. Includes McCann Worldgroup, Lowe, DraftFCB as part of the advertising agencies.
7. Dentsu has a 15 per cent voting stake in Publicis Group via Dentsu's 22 per cent interest in the former Bcom3 Group.
8. Includes Daiko Advertising, formerly ranked 16 in 2001, and Yomiko Advertising, formerly ranked 22 in 2001.
9. A Canadian agency with marketing-communications services and worldwide offices. Its revenue is mainly from the US.
10. Microsoft purchased the digital advertising and marketing services group in 2007.
11. An Australian agency which was founded by Tim Hughes and Simon Reynolds in 2000.
12. A South Korean agency.
13. IBM set this up as a digital-agency services business using IBMÆs expertise of technologies and techniques to facilitate optimal human connection.
14. Founded in 1990. It is a global consulting and technology-services company that markets its services via digital and business and information technologies.
15. 47 per cent owned by Omnicom's BBDO.
16. A Swedish advertising agency.
17. Marketing communications holding company founded in 2000 with a global network.
18. Interbrand 'Best Global Brand 2012. [Online]. Available at: http://www.interbrand.com/en/best-global-brands/2012/downloads.aspx. [Last accessed 30th December 2012]. Interbrand uses a methodology, which is based on three components: namely, analyses of the financial performance of the branded products or services, of the role the brand plays in the purchase decision, and of the competitive strength of the brand.
19. Advertising Association (2004) *The Marketing Pocket Book 2004*. Henley-on-Thames, England: Advertising Association and World Advertising Research Centre.
20. 'Top 50 Global Technology Companies'. [Online]. Available at: http://www.computerwire.com/companies/lists/list/?listid=7A7B551F-A6C8-47AC-B3AE-3879873B5E23. [Last accessed 31st December 2012].
21. 'Global Software Top 100—Edition 2011. [Online]. Available at: http://www.softwaretop100.org/global-software-top-100-edition-2011. [Last accessed 31st December 2012].

About the Author

Dr. Sai Loo is an academic at UCL Institute of Education, University College London. Before joining the Institute, he taught accounting and finance at higher education institutions on undergraduate, postgraduate and professional programmes, and vocational areas in further education. Sai has worked in industry as a Chartered Accountant. His areas of interests are in the interdisciplinary approaches to defining, identifying, and applying knowledge in settings relating to work, learning, and teaching. He has published widely in international refereed journals and some of these can be accessed at ioe.academia.edu/SaiLoo. His recent research monograph by Routledge was *Vocationalism in Further and Higher Education: Policy, programmes and pedagogy.*

Bibliography

Aitchison, J. (2001). *Cutting Edge Commercials: How to Create the World's Best TV Ads for Brands in the 21st Century.* Singapore: Prentice Hall.

Alvesson, M. (2004). *Knowledge Work and Knowledge-Intensive Firms.* Oxford: Oxford University Press.

Ashton, D., Davies, B., Felstead, A. and Green, F. (1999). *Work Skills in Britain.* Warwick University, Warwick: The Centre on Skills, Knowledge and Organisational Performance (SKOPE).

Barron, F. (1983). 'Creative Writers'. In R. S. Albert (Ed.), *Genius and Eminence: The Social Psychology of Creativity and Exceptional Achievement.* Oxford: Pergamon Press Limited, pp. 302–310.

Bateson, G. (1973). *Steps to an Ecology of Mind.* London: Paladin.

Bell, D. (1973). *The Coming of Post-Industrial Society: A Venture in Social Forecasting.* New York: Basic Books.

Bell, D. (1976). *The Coming of Post-Industrial Society: A Venture in Social Forecasting.* New York: Basic Books.

Bennett, N., Dunne, E. and Carre, C. (1999). 'Patterns of core and generic skill provision in higher education'. *Higher Education,* 37(1), 71–93.

Bradburn, N. and Sudman, S. (1979). *Improving Interview Method and Questionnaire Design.* San Francisco: Jossey-Bass.

British Broadcasting Corporation (BBC) (2007). 'Bill Gates: The skills you need to succeed'. *BBC News.* [Online]. Available at: http://news.bbc.co.uk/go/pr/fr/-/2/hi/business/7142073. [Last accessed 14th December 2007].

Brown, P., Green, A. and Lauder, H. (2001). *High Skills: Globalisation, Competitiveness and Skills Formation.* Oxford: Oxford University Press.

Brown, P., Lauder, H. and Ashton, D. (2011). *The Global Auction: The Broken Promises of Education, Jobs and Incomes.* Oxford: Oxford University Press.

Bruner, J. S. (1996). *The Culture of Education.* Cambridge, MA: Harvard University Press.

Burton-Jones, A. (1999). *Knowledge Capitalism: Business, Work, and Learning in the New Economy.* Oxford: Oxford University Press.

Cappo, J. (2003). *The Future of Advertising: New Media, New Clients, New Consumers in the Post-Television Age.* New York: McGraw-Hill.

Castells, M. (2000). *The Information Age: Economy, Society and Culture, Volume 1 The Rise of the Network Society.* Oxford: Blackwell Publishers Limited.

Chaiklin, S. and Lave, J. (1996). *Understanding Practice: Perspectives on Activity and Context.* Cambridge: Cambridge University Press.

Cohen, L., Manion, L. and Morrison, K. (2000). *Research Methods in Education.* London: RoutledgeFalmer.

Cole, M. (1996). *Cultural Psychology: A Once and Future Discipline.* Cambridge, MA: The Belknap Press of Harvard University Press.

Commission of the European Communities (2007). *Communication from the Commission to the European Parliament, the Council, the European Economic and Social Committee and the Committee of the Regions, The European Interest: Succeeding in the Age of Globalization.* Brussels: Contribution of the Commission to the October Meeting of Heads of State and Government, 3.10.2007 COM (2007) 581 final. [Online]. Available at: http:// eurlex.europa.eu.eu/LexUriServ/LexUrServ.do?uri=COM:2007:0581:FIN:EN:PDF. [Last accessed 26th November 2009].

Cortada, J. (1998). *Rise of the Knowledge Worker (Resources for the Knowledge-Based Economy).* Maryland Heights, MO: Butterworth-Heinemann.

Couch, C., Finegold, D. and Sako, M. (1999). *Are Skills the Answer? The Political Economy of Skills Creation in Advanced Industrial Countries.* Oxford: Oxford University Press.

Csikszentmihalyi, M. (1988). 'Society, Culture, and Person: A Systems View of Creativity'. In R. J. Sternberg (Ed.), *The Nature of Creativity.* New York: Cambridge University Press, pp. 325–339.

Cusumano, M. A. and Selby, R. W. (1997). *Microsoft Secrets: How the World's Most Powerful Software Company Creates Technology, Shapes Markets, and Manages People.* London: HarperCollinsBusiness.

Davenport, T. H. (2005). *Thinking for a Living: How to Get Better Performance and Results from Knowledge Workers.* Boston: Harvard Business School Press.

Defillippi, R., Arthur, M. and Lindsay, V. (2006). *Knowledge at Work: Creative Collaboration in the Global Economy.* Hoboken, NJ: Wiley-Blackwell.

Dench, S. (1998). *Keeping IT Together: Skills for Information Technologists.* Brighton, Sussex: The Institute for Employment Studies.

Denscombe, M. (1998). *The Good Research Guide for Small-Scale Social Research Projects.* Buckingham, UK: Open University Press.

Denzin, N. K. (1989). *The Research Act.* Englewood Cliffs, NJ: Prentice Hall.

Department for Culture, Media and Sport (DCMS) (2001). *Creative Industries Mapping Document 2001. (Government Document).* London: DCMS.

Department for Trade and Industry (DTI) (1998). *Our Competitive Future: Building the Knowledge Driven Economy.* London: DTI.

Douglas, J. D. (1985). *Creative Interviewing.* Beverley Hills, CA: Sage.

Drucker, P. (1993). *Post-Capitalist Society.* Oxford: Butterworth Heinemann.

Drucker, P. (1994). *The Age of Discontinuity: Guidelines to Our Changing Society.* New Brunswick, NJ and London: Transaction Publishers.

Drucker, P. (1999). 'Knowledge-worker productivity: The biggest challenge'. *California Management Review,* 41(2), 79–94.

Economist (2003). 'Coming of age: A survey of the IT industry'. *Economist,* 10–16 May 2003.

European Union Commission (2000). *Memorandum on Lifelong Learning.* Brussels: European Union.

Farrell, L. and Fenwick, T. (2007). *World Yearbook of Education: Educating the Global Workforce: Knowledge, Knowledge Work and Knowledge Workers.* Abingdon: Routledge.

Feldman, D. (1980). *Beyond Universals in Cognitive Development.* Norwood, NJ: Ablex.

Feldman, D. and Goldsmith, L. (1986). *Nature's Gambit: Child Prodigies and the Development of Human Potential.* New York: Basic Books.

Florida, R. (2003). *The Rise of the Creative Class: And How It's Transforming Work, Leisure, Community and Everyday Life*. New York: Basic Books.

Franklin, J. and Wray, R. (2008). 'Less killing, more kissing: New breed of computer games bring people together'. *Guardian Newspaper*. [Online]. Available at: http://www.guardian.co.uk/technology/2008/dec/29/spcial-network-games-playfish-facebook/print. [Last accessed 29th December 2008].

Fuller, M. (1984). 'Dimensions of Gender in a School: Reinventing the Wheel?' In R. G. Burgess (Ed.), *The Research Process in Educational Settings: Ten Case Studies*. London: Falmer Press, pp. 97–116.

Gardner, H. (1984). *Frames of Mind: The Theory of Multiple Intelligences*. London: William Heinemann Limited.

Gardner, H. (1993). *Frames of Mind: The Theory of Multiple Intelligences*. London: Fontana Press.

Gardner, H. (1999). *Intelligence Reframed: Multiple Intelligences for the 21st Century*. New York: Basic Books.

Gates, B., Myhrvold, N. and Rinearson, P. (1996). *The Road Ahead*. London: Penguin Books.

Gibson, O. (2005). 'Arctic Monkeys climbing high—thanks to the net'. *Guardian Newspaper*, 17 October 2005. [Online]. Available at: http://arts.guardian.co.uk/news/story/0,11711,1593705,00.html. [Last accessed 17th October 2005].

Grabher, G. (2004). 'Learning in projects, remembering in networks?: Communality, sociality and connectivity in project ecologies'. *European Urban and Regional Studies*, 11, 103–123.

Green, F. (2005). *Demanding Work: The Paradox of Job Quality in the Affluent Economy*. Princeton, NJ: Princeton University Press.

Guile, D. (2006). 'What Is Distinctive about the Knowledge Economy? Implications for Education'. In H. Lauder, P. Brown, J.-A. Dillabough and A. H. Halsey (Eds.), *Globalisation, Education and the Social Change*. Oxford: Oxford University Press, pp. 355–366.

Guile, D. (2010). *The Learning Challenge of the Knowledge Economy*. Rotterdam: Sense Publishers.

Herbig, P. and Jacobs, L. (1996). 'Creative problem-solving styles in the USA and Japan'. *International Marketing Review*, 13(2), 63–71.

Hoch, D. J., Roeding, G., Purkert, G. and Lindner, S. K. (1999). *Secrets of Software Success: Management Insights from 100 Software Firms Around the World*. Boston, MA: Harvard Business School Press.

Howkins, J. (2001). *The Creative Economy: How People Make Money from Ideas*. London: Penguin Books.

Jemielniak, D. (2012). *The New Knowledge Worker*. Cheltenham: Edward Elgar.

Jones, J. P. (Ed.) (1999). *How to Use Advertising to Build Strong Brands*. Thousand Oaks, CA: Sage Publications Incorporated.

Kao, J. J. (1991). *Managing Creativity*. Englewood Cliffs, NJ: Prentice Hall.

Kirton, M. (1976). 'Adaptors and innovators: A description and measure'. *Journal of Applied Psychology*, 61(5), 622–629.

Klein, L. (2008). *The Meaning of Work: Papers on Work Organization and the Design of Jobs*. London: Karnac Books.

Klein, N. (2001). *No Logo*. London: Flamingo.

Knorr Cetina, K. (1997). 'Sociality with objects'. *Theory, Culture and Society*, 14, 1–30.

Knorr Cetina, K. (2001a). 'Transitions in Post-Social Knowledge Societies'. In B. Ben-Rafael and Y. Sternberg (Eds.), *Identity, Culture and Globalization*. Leiden/Boston/Koln: Brill, pp. 611–628.

Knorr Cetina, K. (2001b). 'Objectual Practice'. In T. Schatzki, K. Knorr Cetina and E. Savigny (Eds.), *The Practice Turn in Contemporary Theory*. London: Routledge, pp. 175–188.

Knorr Cetina, K. and Bruegger, U. (2002a). 'Global microstructures: The virtual societies of financial markets'. *American Journal of Sociology*, 107(4), 905–950.

Knorr Cetina, K. and Bruegger, U. (2002b). 'Traders' engagement with markets: A post-social relationship'. *Theory, Culture and Society*, 19(5–6), 161–185.

Knorr Cetina, K. (2005a). 'Culture in Global Knowledge Societies: Knowledge Cultures and Epistemic Cultures'. In M. D. Jacobs and N. W. Hanrahan (Eds.), *The Blackwell Companion to the Sociology of Culture*. Malden, MA /Oxford/Carlton, Victoria, Australia: Blackwell Publishing Limited, pp. 65–79.

Knorr Cetina, K. (2005b). 'Science, Technology and Their Implications'. In C. Calhoun, C. Rojak and B. Turner (Eds.), *The Sage Handbook of Sociology*. London/Thousand Oaks, CA/New Delhi: Sage Publications Limited, pp. 546–560.

Krotoski, A. (2008). 'Calling all budding game developers'. *Guardian Newspaper*, 30 April 2008. [Online]. Available at: http://www.guardian.co.uk/2008/apr/30/textadventure/print. [Last accessed 30th April 2008].

Lash, S. and Urry, J. (1994). *Economics of Signs and Space*. London: Sage Publications Limited.

Law, A. (2001). *Open Minds: 21st Century Business Lessons and Innovations from St Luke's*. London: Texere Publishing Limited.

Loo, S. (2011). 'A re-assessment of knowledge from the perspective of the knowledge economy'. *The International Journal of the Humanities*, 9(2), 111–120.

Lury, C. (2004). *Brands: The Logos of the Global Economy*. London and New York: Routledge.

MacKinnon, D. W. (1962). *The Personality Correlates of Creativity: A Study of American Architects*. Proceedings of the Fourteenth Congress on Applied Psychology, vol. 2, Munksgaard, Copenhagen, Denmark, pp. 11–39.

MacLennan, B. J. (2008). 'Aesthetics in Software Engineering'. In M. Khosrow-Pour (Ed.), *Encyclopedia of Information Science and Technology*, Vol. 1. New York: IGI Global.

Martinez-Fernandez, C., Miles, I. and Weyman, T. (2011). *The Knowledge Economy at Work: Skills and Innovation in Knowledge Intensive Service Activities*. Cheltenham: Edward Elgar Publishing Ltd.

Miles, M. B. and Hubermann, A. M. (1994). *Qualitative Data Analysis: An Expanded Sourcebook*. Thousand Oaks, CA: Sage.

Miller, C. (1995). 'In-depth interviewing by telephone: Some practical considerations'. *Evaluation and Research in Education*, 9(1), 29–38.

Ministry of Trade and Industry (MTI) (1998). *Committee on Singapore's Competitiveness*. Singapore: MTI.

Moschella, D. (2003). *Customer-Driven IT*. Harvard: Harvard Business School Press.

National Advisory Committee on Creative and Cultural Education (NACCCE) (1999). *All Our Futures: Creativity, Culture and Education. (Government Document)*. London: Department for Education and Employment.

Nerland, M. (2008). 'Knowledge cultures and the shaping of work-based learning: The case of computer engineering'. *Vocations and Learning*, 1, 49–69.

Nonaka, I. and Takeuchi, H. (1995). *The Knowledge Creating Company: How Japanese Companies Create the Dynamics of Innovation*. New York: Oxford University Press.

Ogilvy, D. (2003). *Ogilvy on Advertising*. London: Prion Books.

Oppenheim, A. N. (1992). *Questionnaire Design, Interviewing and Attitude Measurement*. London: Heinemann.

Organization for Economic Co-operation and Development (OECD) (1996). *Lifelong Learning for All*. Paris: OECD.

Organization for Economic Co-operation and Development (OECD) (2002). *ICTs and the Information Economy*. Paris: OECD.

O'Riain, S. (2004). 'Net-Working for a Living: Irish Software Developers in the Global Workplace'. In A. Amin and N. Thrift (Eds.), *The Blackwell Cultural Economy Reader*. Malden, MA: Blackwell Publishing Limited, pp. 15–39.

Orr, K., Nutley, S., Russell, S., Bain, R., Hacking, E. and Moran, C. (2016). *Knowledge and Practice in Business and Organisations*. Abingdon: Routledge.

Oxford University Press (1990). *The Concise Oxford Dictionary*. Oxford: Oxford University Press.

Patton, M. Q. (1980). *Qualitative Evaluation Methods*. Beverly Hills: Sage Publications.

Polanyi, M. (1966). *The Tacit Dimension*. London: Routledge and Kegan Paul.

Poon, J. T. F. (1998). 'Creativity in business and innovative organisations'. *Industry and Higher Education*, 12(2), 84–92.

Quah, D. (1999). *Growth and Increasingly Weightless Economies*. Paper presented at the Economics of the Knowledge Driven Economy conference. Department of Trade and Industry and the Centre for Economic Policy Research, London. 27th January 1999.

Quah, D. (2002). *Digital Goods and the New Economy*. London: Centre for Economic Performance, London School of Economics. [Online]. Available at: http://cep.lse.ac.uk/pubs/download/dp0563.pdf. [Last accessed 29th November 2005].

Reich, R. B. (2001). *The Future of Success: Work and Life in the New Economy*. London: William Heinemann.

Reinhardt, W., Schmidt, B., Sloep, P. and Drachsler, H. (2011). 'Knowledge worker roles and actions—results of two empirical studies'. *Knowledge and Process Management*, 18(3), 150–174.

Resnick, L. B. (1987). *Education and Learning to Think*. Washington, DC: National Academy Press.

Richardson, K. (1991). *Understanding Intelligence*. Philadelphia: Open University Press.

Robson, C. (2002). *Real World Research*. Malden, MA: Blackwell Publishing.

Sawyer, K. (2007). *Group Genius: The Creative Power of Collaboration*. New York: Basic Books.

Schiesel, S. (2008). 'In top-selling games, a turn toward the social'. *Money Business, New York Times*, 16 March 2008, p. 5.

Smolucha, F. (1993). 'Review of multiple intelligences: The theory in practice'. *Choice*, 31(2), 368.

Smyth, J. and Shacklock, G. (1998). 'Behind the "Cleansing" of Socially Critical Research Accounts'. In G. Shacklock and J. Smyth (Eds.), *Being Reflexive in Critical Educational and Social Research*. London: Falmer Press, pp. 1–12.

Spradley, J. P. (1979). *The Ethnographic Interview*. New York: Holt, Rinehart and Winston.

Sternberg, R. J., Kaufman, J. C. and Pretz, J. E. (2004). 'A propulsion model of creative leadership'. *Creativity and Innovation Management*, 13(3), 145–153.

Sweney, M. (2009). 'Internet overtakes television to become biggest advertising sector in the UK'. *Guardian Newspaper*, 30 September 2009. [Online]. Available at: http://www.guardian.co.uk/media/2009/sep30/Internet-biggest uk-advertising-secot/print. [Last accessed 30th September 2009].

Thompson, H. (1985). *Hell's Angels*. New York: Ballantine.

Tizard, B. and Hughes, M. (1996). 'Reflections on Young Children Learning'. In G. Walford (Ed.), *Doing Educational Research*. London: Routledge, pp. 19–40.

Torvalds, L. and Diamond, D. (2001). *Just for Fun: The Story of an Accidental Revolutionary*. New York & London: Texere.

Vaske, H. (2001). *Standing on the Shoulders of Giants: Herman Vaske's Conversations with the Masters of Advertising*. Berlin: Die Gestalten Verlag.

Victor, B. and Boynton, A. C. (1998). *Invented Here: Maximizing Your Organization's Internal Growth and Profitability*. Boston, MA: Harvard Business School Press.

Virgo, P. (2001). *What Skills Shortages? 2001 IT Skills Trend Report Revised, Management Summary Only (V2 8/1/01)*. Orpington, England: Institute for the Management of Information Systems (IMIS) and the Computer Weekly 500 Club.

von Hippel, E. V. (2006). *Democratizing Innovation*. Cambridge, MA: The Massachusetts Institute of Technology Press.

Walford, G. (1987). 'Introduction: The Research Process'. In G. Walford (Ed.), *Doing Sociology of Education*. London: Falmer Press, pp. 1–7.

Waterhouse, L. (2006). 'Inadequate evidence for multiple intelligences, mozart effect, and emotional intelligence theories'. *Educational Psychologists*, 41(4), 247–255.

Wax, R. (1960). 'Twelve Years Later: An Analysis of Field Experiences'. In R. N. Adams and J. J. Preiss (Eds.), *Human Organizational Research: Field Relations and Techniques*. Homewood, IL: Dorsey.

White, J. (1998). *Do Howard Gardner's Multiple Intelligences Add Up?* London: Institute of Education, University of London.

Winslow, C. D. and Branmer, W. L. (1994). *FutureWork: Putting Knowledge to Work in the Knowledge Economy*. London: Simon and Schuster.

Zuboff, S. (1988). *In the Age of the Smart Machine: The Future of Work and Power*. Oxford: Heinemann Professional Publishing.

Zuboff, S. (2004). 'Managing the Informated Organization'. In F. Webster (Ed.), *The Information Society Reader*. New York & London: Routledge, pp. 313–328.

Index

Made in the USA
Las Vegas, NV
30 November 2021